TAKE *and* EAT

GREAT CHRISTIAN BOOKS

LINDENHURST, NEW YORK

TAKE *and* EAT

VINCENT ROTOLO

A GREAT CHRISTIAN BOOKS publication
Great Christian Books is an imprint of Rotolo Media
160 37th Street Lindenhurst, New York 11757 (631) 956-0998
www.GreatChristianBooks.com
email: mail@greatchristianbooks.com
Take and Eat   ISBN 978-161010-025-0

Rotolo, Vincent, 1940-
Take and Eat / by Vincent Rotolo
p. cm.
A "A Great Christian Book" book
GREAT CHRISTIAN BOOKS a division of Rotolo Media
ISBN 978-161010-025-0
Recommended Dewey Decimal Classifications: 204, 230, 234
Suggested Subject Headings:
1. Religion—Christian literature—Worldview
2. Christianity—The Bible—Practical Theology
I. Title

Scripture quotations are from the King James Bible unless
otherwise noted. Italicized words in scripture quotations are
the emphasis of the author.

The book and cover design for this title are by Michael Rotolo.
It is typeset in the Minion and Myriad typefaces by Adobe Inc.
and is manufactured in the United States on acid-free stock.
To discuss the publication of your Christian manuscript or to
republish your out-of-print book, contact Great Christian Books.

To my family and friends—
I pray that we all meet in heaven.

—Vin

Contents

INTRODUCTION

Dear Friends,

I begin this book with what I call *My Tract*. Years ago, as a young Christian I had put this tract together and printed a thousand to hand out to everyone I knew. I had to to tell them the good news. You'll see it is composed largely of my favorite verses from the Bible. I believe that Jesus and the Word of God are synonymous. The Bible says that Jesus is the very Word of God come to life. So the Word expressed in the gospel (good news) of Jesus Christ and accompanied by the Holy Spirit, is all that one needs to know Jesus Christ. If you're already a Christian these verses should strengthen and encourage you. If you're not, then consider this my friend,— God has put this book before you for a reason. This truth must be taught and Jesus wants those of us who know it to make disciples of others. This truth must be shared faithfully for it is often misunderstood.

God says that real faith comes by hearing the Word of God and that this faith will save us from our sinful condition and unite us to God forever. It is necessary to save us and necessary to mature us to live a holy life for God. The question remains will you respond to God's call to believe these things? If you happen to be one of those folks into whose hands I personally put this book then you can trust that I am praying for you personally by name! I love you and want you to become acquainted with my Savior. He has been so good to me that I must share this with you. This is the best gift I could ever give you!

I hope you'll be blessed by my effort to share the word of God with you who perhaps by the grace of God may hear it and live. Some of you will be bored to death by a story you've never really heard or understood. Some of you think you know it, but please bear with me, and give me the chance to explain it to you again. You see it pleases God by the preaching of His Word to save those that are lost. This life is the only chance you will get at eternal bliss. I implore you not to waste this opportunity. Jesus said that the Word is with you for only a little while, and commands that while there is light we are to walk in that light. We all start this life equally; God describes us as lost, blind, and dead in our sins, until He who is rich in mercy, supernaturally enters into the hearts of men and women and causes them to realize their need for a Savior. My prayer is that those of you who do not intimately know Jesus Christ as the Lord of All will be among those many blessed souls that come to know Him and grow in grace and truth. Remember we are all by nature lost sheep led astray by our imaginations and by false ideas. God knows that we will never seek Him or His salvation alone, and so he promises:

> "*I will gather* the remaining of my flock out of all the countries where I have driven them, and will bring them again to their folds, and they shall be fruitful and increase. And *I will set up shepherds* over them *which shall feed them*, and they shall fear no more...says the Lord." —Jer 23:3-4

God will do it—He will gather. He is God who cannot lie. He invites you...

> "You will seek me and find me, when you seek me with all your heart." —Jer 29:13 (ESV)

He loves to feed His sheep. The method He uses to feed us is to declare the works and words of His Son Jesus Christ. You are fed by reading the Bible and by hearing good preaching from faithful shepherds.

The balance of this book is a collection of many of my essays from years of contributing to what were known at my church as *The Shepherd's Notes*. These were a few short pages written to the congregation each week while I served as an elder. Each week a different elder would take a turn feeding the sheep at our church by writing an essay. So about once a month I was called to bring a word of instruction, admonition, or encouragement to the church through my *Shepherd's Note*. I've collected together thirty of my favorites to share with you. They've been edited and expanded so they will be relevant and helpful to you.

It should become apparent that I rely upon God's Word as the only true guide for life and believe every word can be trusted. God's words are the power by which He communicates deep, life-changing truths—so whenever possible I use a Bible quotation to show you directly from Scripture the idea I'm sharing. It's always best to hear it directly as God has said it so it would be helpful to read this with a Bible at hand so you can reference the verses I use as examples. Reading the verses that surround them helps to give you the context and will aid in understanding. Remember these truths are not my opinions but come right out of God's Word. The Bible glorifies God, and places Him on the highest throne. True teaching keeps Him raised high on that throne, while error (usually the idea that we contribute to our salvation) brings Him down and makes Him a failure, or at best, one who's made a valiant attempt but needs our help to complete it. Such error, exalts the creature and not the Creator. Why did Jesus need to die if we could do something to save ourselves? If our morality or religion or sacrifices could save us, then why would Christ sacrifice Himself to save sinners? Read on and you will receive the answers to these questions.

If you find something I'm saying strikes you as new, different, odd or just plain wrong, as far as you're concerned, I urge you to open your Bible and do your own reading. By all means, test what I've written against what the Bible says. God would be pleased that you did. Don't simply accept what I've written because you assume I'm an authority on the Bible— I want you to become acquainted with it through your own reading. If you're new to the Bible I've included a guide at the back of this book to the abbreviations that are used for the books of the Bible whenever I quote it.

These essays are written in a conversational tone so I find it helpful to emphasize certain words in the Bible verses I'm quoting by using *italics*. There are rarely italics in the Bible itself, I just do this to bring your attention to particular words relevant to the idea we're discussing. The King James version of the Bible is my preference, I enjoy the Old English. It's an excellent translation but you can use a different translation to follow along. As you'll see, the truth is still the same even if the wording is slightly different.

I'm praying that this book will be a real blessing to you. Between my tract and over thirty *Shepherd's Notes* you have a little more than a month's worth of devotional reading. So... Take and Eat!

May God Bless you,

Vin

"Thy words were found, *and I did eat them*; and thy Word was unto me the joy and rejoicing of mine heart: for I am called by thy name, O LORD God of hosts." —Jeremiah 15:16

"How sweet *are your words unto my taste*! yea, sweeter than honey to my mouth!" — Psalm 119:103

MY TRACT

For I am not ashamed

of the gospel of Christ,

for it is the power

of God unto Salvation.

—Romans 1:16

The fool has said in his heart, there is no God. —Psalm 14:1

Examine me, O Lord and prove me, try my mind, and my heart. —Psalm 26:2

Show me Thy ways, O Lord, teach me Thy paths. —Psalm 25:4,5

Lead me in Thy truth, and teach me for Thou are the God of my salvation; O keep my soul, and deliver me: let me not be ashamed: for I put my trust in Thee. —Psalm 25:20

Teach me Thy way, O Lord. —Psalm 27:11

It pleased God by the foolishness of preaching to save them that believed. —1 Corinthians 1:21

Go ye into all the world, and preach the gospel to every creature. He that believeth and is baptized shall be saved; but he that believeth not shall be damned. —Mark 16:15, 16

So then faith cometh by hearing, and hearing by the word of God. —Romans 10:17

Search the Scriptures; for in them ye think ye have eternal life; and they are they which testify of Me. —John 5:39

Verily, verily, I say unto you, he that heareth My word, and believeth on Him that sent Me, hath everlasting life, and shall not come into condemnation, but is passed from death unto life. — John 5:24

Heaven and earth shall pass away: but My words shall not pass away. —Mark 13:31

If a man love Me, he will keep My words, and My Father will love him, and We will come unto him, and make Our abode with him. —John 14:23

For whosoever shall be ashamed of Me and My words, of him shall the Son of Man be ashamed. —Luke 9:26

Have mercy upon me, O Lord, for I am in trouble. —Psalm 31:9

Good and upright is the Lord: therefore will He teach sinners in the way. —Psalm 25:8

For all have sinned, and come short of the glory of God.
                                        —Romans 3:23

There is none righteous, no not one. —Romans 3:10

If we say we have no sin we deceive ourselves, and the truth is not in us. —1 John 1:8

But we are all as an unclean thing, and all our righteousness are as filthy rags. —Isa 64:6

For there is not a just man upon earth, that doeth good, and sinneth not. —Ecc 7:20

So then every one of us shall give account of himself to God. —Romans 14:12

And as it is appointed unto men once to die, but after this the judgment. —Hebrews 9:27

For the wages of sin is death; but the gift of God is eternal life through Jesus Christ our Lord. —Romans 6:23

The fear of the Lord is the beginning of knowledge. —Prv 1:7

And I saw the dead, small and great, stand before God; and the books were opened, which is the book of life; and the dead were judged out of those things which were written in the books, according to their works. —Revelation 20:12

Wherefore, as by one man sin entered into the world, and death by sin; and so death passed upon all men, for that all have sinned. —Romans 5:12

The soul that sinneth, it shall die. —Ezekiel 18:20

The wicked shall be turned into hell. —Psalm 9:17

Put them in fear O Lord. —Psalm 9:20

Have mercy upon me, O God, according to Thy loving kindness: according unto the multitude of Thy tender mercies blot out my transgressions. Wash me thoroughly from mine iniquity, and cleanse me from my sin. —Psalm 51:1, 2

Then will I sprinkle clean water upon you, and ye shall be clean: from all your filthiness, and from all your idols, will I cleanse you. A new heart also will I give you, and a new spirit will I put within you: and I will take away the stoney heart out of your flesh, and I will give you a heart of flesh. And I will put my spirit within you and cause you to walk in My statutes, and ye shall keep My judgements, and do them. And ye shall dwell in the land that I gave to your fathers; and ye shall be My people, and I will be your God. —Ezekiel 36:25-28

Now we are clean through the word which I have spoken unto you. —John 15:3

So then it is not of him that willeth nor of him that runneth, but of God that sheweth mercy. —Romans 9:16

I will have mercy on whom I will have mercy, and I will have compassion on whom I will have compassion. —Romans 9:15

Have mercy upon me O God... For I acknowledge my transgressions: and my sin is ever before me. —Psalm 51:3

What will ye? shall I come unto you with a rod, or in love, and in the spirit of meekness.—1 Corinthians 4:21

What must I do to be saved? Believe on the Lord Jesus Christ, and thou shall be saved, and thy house. —Acts 76:30, 31

For whosoever shall call upon the name of the Lord shall be saved. —Romans 10:13

That if thou shalt confess with my mouth the Lord Jesus, and shall believe in thine heart that God hath raised him from the dead, thou shalt be saved. —Romans 10:9

Neither is there salvation in any other: for there is none other name under heaven given among men, whereby we must be saved. —Acts 4:12

Repent ye therefore, and be converted, that your sins may be blotted out. —Acts 3:19

But God demonstrates his love towards us, in that, while we were yet sinners, Christ died for us. —Romans 5:8

For God so loved the world, that He gave His only begotten Son, that whosoever believeth in Him should not perish, but have everlasting life. —John 3:16

Take heed unto thyself, and unto the doctrine; continue in them: for in doing this thou shalt both save thyself, and them that hear thee. —1 Timothy 4:16

For by grace are ye saved through faith; and that not of yourselves: it is a gift of God: not of works, lest any man should boast.
—Ephesians 2:8,9

For He hath made Him to be sin for us, who knew no sin; that we might be made the righteousness of God in Him.
—2 Corinthians 5:21

Who His own self bare our sins in His own body on the tree, that we, being dead to sins should live unto righteousness: by whose stripes ye were healed. —1 Peter 2:24

Greater love hath no man than this, that a man lay down his life for his friend. —John 15:13

Ye must be born again. —John 3:7

Whosoever shall confess Me before men, him will I confess also before My Father which is in heaven. —Matthew 10:32

All that the Father giveth Me shall come to Me, and him that cometh to Me I will by no means cast out. —John 6:37

For what shall it profit a man, if he shall gain the whole world, and lose his own soul? —Mark 8:36

For Thou desirest not sacrifice, else would I give it: Thou delightest not in burnt offering. The sacrifices of God are a broken spirit: a broken and a contrite heart. O God Thou wilt not despise.
—Psalm 51:16,17

Ask, and it shall be given you; seek, and ye shall find; knock, and it shall be opened unto you. —Luke 11:9

Behold, I stand at the door, and knock: if any man hear My voice, and open the door, I will come into him, and he with Me. To him that overcometh will I grant to sit with Me in My throne, even as I also overcame, and am set down with My Father in His throne. He that hath an ear, let him hear. —Rev. 3:20,21,22

Who shall separate us from the love of Christ? shall tribulation, or distress, or persecution, or famine, or nakedness, or peril, or sword? For I am persuaded, that neither death, nor life, nor angels, nor principalities, nor powers, nor things present, nor things to come, nor height, nor depth, nor any other creature, shall be able to separate us from the love of God, which is in Christ Jesus our Lord. —Romans 8:35,38,39

Most Gracious Heavenly Father,

I pray it be your will that what I write will soften hearts, give ears to hear, and eyes to see the magnificence of your word and your plan of salvation. I love you because you first loved me, when I was unworthy of that love. You chose me as I sought in vain to earn my place in heaven.

Thank you for your gift of eternal life which you graciously gave, not only to me but to my wife and children. Less of me and more of Thee, I pray in the blessed name of Jesus.

Some time ago my Dad explained that he had read that a man is not fully educated until he has read the Bible. Well, thank you Dad and thank you Lord. And so I read. What an education! God is a great teacher. What a temporal state in which we exist. I learned I was going to live eternally: either happy with the Lord in heaven, or continue dead in my sins in hell. All my efforts through prayer, church, sacraments, all fell short of God's righteousness.

My eyes started to open. By God's standard, we can never do good enough, and the law we try to obey was put here to show us our sin and failures. We can't make it without divine help. It is what Jesus did on the cross. His death for our sins, and the fact that He suffered hell in our stead which enables us to stand before God. We are cloaked with the righteousness of Christ and God remembers our sin no more.

God chose us, we did not choose Him. Salvation is a free gift, one we could never earn, for all fall short of the glory of God and there is not one who is righteous, no not one.

My ears were hearing. Friends and family— there are no churches in heaven, no Baptists, Presbyterians, Protestants, or Roman Catholics. Only the children of God who trusted on Jesus and what He accomplished on the cross inherit heaven and are born from above. The Bible declares that we are on our way to hell... and shows us our Savior and the path to heaven.

Both our dilemma and solution are revealed.

God says, "My people perish from lack of knowledge." That knowledge along with faith, comes from hearing, and hearing from the word of God... the Bible. God left His word for us to test our beliefs against His truth: to prove all things and hold fast to truth.

Jesus said, "The words I speak unto you, they are spirit and they are life." The words, the life, Jesus, the Bible, the truth are all the same. Please start reading so that God can reach you, and while you do, pray that our Sovereign God will have pity on you and save you from hell. Cling only to the cross, and not to tradition, belief, religion, nor deed.

"I am the good shepherd and know My sheep, and am known of Mine. As the Father knoweth Me, even so know I the Father: and I lay down My life for the sheep. And other sheep I have which are not of this fold: them also I must bring, and they shall hear My voice; and then shall be one fold, and one shepherd." John 10:14-16

My prayer is that you trust in that Shepherd.

"These things have I written unto you that believe on the name of the Son of God: that ye may know that ye have eternal life, and that ye may believe on the name of the Son of God." —John 5:13

Yes the Bible even assures us.

Thank you for giving me the opportunity of sharing my gift with you. Please reread the scriptural portion when you have some quiet uninterrupted time to spend with the Lord.

For those of you who do not know how to begin praying to God consider this as a simple prayer to begin with as a suggestion:

Dear God,

I know I am a sinner because I have broken your laws and that I deserve your wrath in hell. I know that I am unable to save myself. Please save me!

I believe that the death of Christ is sufficient to pay for my sins and make me righteous before you.

I believe that your Word is truth.

Please grant me the free gift of eternal life.

Be my Savior and Lord, Save me—a sinner, I know only you can!

Amen.

You'll Be Sorry

I don't remember the name of the book, but I'll never forget it's last chapter, for it made me weep.

The story was of a young black man in the deep South, taunted by racist, ignorant "rednecks". One day they kill him. Somehow they are never found guilty and walk freely, despicable as ever, until the day the father of the young man confronts them with a challenge to— "Meet me tomorrow and you'll be sorry." The next day, this gang of fools waits for the old father with rifles and clubs, as they don't know what to expect. The father arrives in his battered pick-up truck, and starts unloading it before them. He takes out oil paintings that his son had created, one more beautiful than the next. They are perplexed and understand nothing in their ignorance. The Father, through his tears, shouts: "I told you would be sorry!" With all the amazing work unappreciated and lying before them, they begin to curse the father with one racial epithet after another. They laugh in their relief and grow zealous in their maligning. The gift they forever destroyed remains outside the grasp of their small, depraved minds.

The father understood the value and gift of his son and the impact of his loss. "For unto us a Child is born, unto us a Son is given." (Isaiah 9:6) The gang of fools understood nothing. "That seeing they might not see and hearing they might not understand." (Mark 4:12) The father although premature in his prediction, was correct— they will be sorry.

I sometimes reflect on the abundance I have been given, and wonder if I will ever be sorry. As one more beautiful painting is set before me, will I respond in obedience and return His love? Do I reject the gift and curse the giver? Am I lukewarm, forgetting my first love? How am I treating the gift of Christ?

In another sense, each of us, if we are a Christian, is an empty canvas. God proceeds to paint a picture by the Holy Spirit's work in our hearts. He paints with the fruit of the Spirit, and I believe we can influence the intensity and brilliance of this work. We have the responsibility to be a painting of encouragement rather than despairing; to be a picture of patience rather than anger.

How is the world to see the resurrected Christ today? How do they behold His glory? Am I truly being a sign and wonder to Israel, as the prophet stated we are to be in Isaiah 8, or am I too often lamenting as the Psalmist who asks in Psalm 88:

> "Wilt Thou show wonders to the dead? Shall the dead arise and praise Thee?...Shall thy lovingkindness be declared in the grave? Or thy faithfulness in destruction? Shall thy wonders be known in the dark and thy righteousness in the land of forgetfulness?

When I stand before my creator will I be sorry? Am I allowing God who began a good work in me to complete it or am I hindering Him? Am I building the church that the gates of hell will not prevail against?

C.S. Lewis observes,

> "Our Lord finds our desires, not too strong, but too weak. We are half-hearted creatures, fooling about with drink and sex and ambition when infinite joy is offered us, like an

ignorant child who wants to go on making mud pies in a slum because he cannot imagine what is meant by the offer of a holiday at sea. We are too easily pleased."

The death of the old man's son at the hands of the rednecks left him only with perpetual sorrow; bereft of joy. The death of God's own Son, on the other hand, has given us every reason to rejoice. We were given joy and not the grief. We have been made to be beautiful paintings of God's grace and should declare to the world— "You'll be sorry!", unless you too embrace the Son. I think the things that hold us back are our worldly preoccupations, which are never truly satisfying or lasting. Winston Churchill said "Success is never final" and we can be certain that no worldly achievements are lasting but what we do for God will endure for all of eternity.

God painted great portraits in Christ: The Door, The Way, The Truth, The Savior, Lamb, Bridegroom, Shepherd, and on and on, one as perfect as the other. We who can see, must insist that we see it in ourselves.

Ponder anew, all the Almighty can do.

Anxious About Your Soul?

"This is the work of God, that ye believe on Him whom He hath sent." —John 6:29

William Reid, a 19th Century Saint may be of some help:

"The Holy Spirit is most essential to your seeing Jesus to the saving of your souls, and your anxious eyes must rest in the fact that 'It is Christ that died.' Rm 8:24 The Spirit directs us to Calvary: 'It is finished.' 'The blood of Jesus Christ His Son cleanseth us from all sin.' We are called to receive Jesus as Redeemer, that we may 'have redemption through His blood, the forgiveness of sins, according to the riches of His grace.' "
                                                                    —Eph 1:7

The blood smeared upon the lintel secured Israel's peace. God saw the blood and passed by. He saw nothing else. We need to rest simply on God's word that the blood is sufficient, a perfect atonement for our sin. We are constantly prone to look at something in ourselves as necessary to form the ground of peace with God. We are more likely to regard the work of the Spirit *in* us rather than the work of Christ *for* us. It was Christ that secured our peace. The Spirit shows us Christ and enables us to enjoy Him.

"He is the author of every holy aspiration in us. No power or energy of the Holy Ghost could cancel sin; the blood has done that." —C. H. Mackintosh

Please see the simplicity of the ground on which your peace is to rest. God is well pleased in the finished work of Christ—

"Until I saw the blood, 'Twas hell my soul was fearing;
And dark and dreary in my eyes' the future was appearing.

While conscience told it's tale of sin,
And caused a weight of woe within.

But when I saw the blood, And looked at Him who shed it,
My right to peace was seen at once, And I with transport read it;

I found myself to God brought nigh,
And "Victory" became my cry.

My joy was in the blood, The news of which had told me,
that spotless as the Lamb of God, My Father could behold me.

And all my boast was in His name,
through whom this great salvation came.

And when, with golden harps, the throne of God surrounding,
the white-robed saints around the throne, their songs of joy are sounding;

With them I'll praise that precious blood,
which has redeem'd our souls to God."

—from *The Blood of Jesus* by William Reid

When we seek an assurance of salvation we need to contemplate that we are saved by what Christ has done, and not by our subjective feelings.

"Therefore, being justified (it's already done) by faith, we have peace with God through our Lord Jesus Christ." —Rm 5:1

No more war with God, not a feeling which can't be trusted, but a promise from a God who cannot lie.

We stand in the presence of a holy God who now gives us access to Him; rejoice (not doubting) in the hope (a concrete knowing) of the glory of God.

You may not always feel saved, and Satan will gladly confirm those feelings of doubt, but God screams at you, "You have been saved, I did it. I am faithful, fear not for I am with thee, be not dismayed, I am thy God, when thou passes through the waters, I will be with thee, I will uphold thee, I am the Hope of Glory, turn your eyes on me, your blessed assurance." We have not been called to doubt, but to holiness.

> "These things have I written unto you that believe on the name of the Son of God, that ye may know that ye have eternal life, and that ye may believe on the name (everything He did and is) of the Son of God." —1 Jn 5:13

This is knowledge or assurance of salvation and eternal life. And, very interesting, in the place of a benediction, he exhorts; "Little children, keep yourselves from idols." Do we nurture our doubt and attempt to cleanse our already cleansed selves— this too can become a false idol! In a never ending state of doubt, we are useless to do God's work. How do we go into all the world, if we feel we are not accepted and must be more worthy? Brother and Sister; we were never, ever worthy.

> "Let us draw near with a true heart in full assurance of faith, having our hearts sprinkled from an evil conscience, and our bodies washed with pure water. Let us hold fast the profession of our faith without wavering, for He is faithful that promised." —Heb 10:22

Christ's sacrifice has done it all. Hold fast, don't waiver: for who can separate us from the love of God?

Grow Old In Wisdom

"The hoary head (gray hair) is a crown of glory, *if* it be found in the way of righteousness." —Proverbs 16:31

Now that's a big— "IF" because the wicked also get gray hair, but none of the godly glory. Only the one who has grown old in the pursuit of wisdom, is crowned with the glory of God's grace... the world on the other hand is, as the saying goes,— "Too soon old, Too late smart!"

We need God's wisdom and doctrine for our present, and eternal lives. Doctrine is teaching, it is what the Apostles passed to us and that which we receive as true about God and mankind.

Paul instructs Timothy, to: "watch your life and your doctrine closely." He tells him: "to let the profiting of it be seen by all." (1 Timothy 4:15,16) Timothy is to continue in this gift that is in him, "for in doing this, thou shall save both thyself, and them that hear thee."

We must understand what the God who lies behind this life is saying, and have a biblical framework by which to operate in the midst of the trials of life. Avoid today's trend of downplaying the importance of doctrine in our lives. Remember that: "Faith, without works, is dead." If our actions continue consistent with our beliefs in discerning truth from error, it will be reflected in our lives. We must manifest the grace and salvation that has been given us.

The very next verse states:

> "He that is slow to anger is better than the mighty; and he that ruleth his spirit than he that taketh a city." —Prv 16:32

I recall recently, doing just the opposite— not being slow to anger, and getting out of control. We are not sinless, but we ought to "sin less". So, when I sin, I go immediately back to the drawing board of God's instruction.

> "Hear, ye children, the instruction of a father, and attend to know understanding. For I give you good doctrine, forsake ye not my law." —Prv 4:1

God's good doctrine must be our only focal point for all instruction, for without it, there is no wisdom.

> "Let thine heart retain my words: keep my commandments and live." — Prv 4:1b

> "Wisdom is the principal thing; therefore *get wisdom*: and with all thy getting get understanding." —Prv 4:7

I love that— "with all thy getting get..." Could there be any clearer and simpler command?

> "Hear O my son, (here is the Father talking to His elect) and receive my sayings; and the years of thy life shall be many." —Prv 4:10

And by *many*, it is not merely meant in this life but hints at eternity.

> "Who is a wise man and endued with knowledge among you? let him shew out of a good conversation his works with *meekness of wisdom*." —Jas 3:13

> "There is wisdom from God, as opposed to earthly, sensual and devilish wisdom, and that is the wisdom we need. It "is

first pure, then peaceable, gentle, and easy to be entreated, full of mercy and good fruits, without partiality, and without hypocrisy." —Jas 3:17

"Now therefore hearken, O Israel, unto the statutes and unto the judgments, which I teach you, for to do them, that ye may live , and go in and possess the land which the LORD God of your fathers giveth you. Ye shall not add unto the word which I command you, neither shall ye diminish ought from it, that ye may keep the commandments of the LORD your God which I command you. Your eyes have seen what the LORD did because of Baalpeor: for all the men that followed Baalpeor, the LORD thy God hath destroyed them from among you. But ye that did cleave unto the LORD your God are alive every one of you this day. Behold , I have taught you statutes and judgments, even as the LORD my God commanded me, that ye should do so in the land whither ye go to possess it. Keep therefore and do them; for *this is your wisdom and your understanding* in the sight of the nations, which shall hear all these statutes, and say, Surely this great nation is *a wise and understanding people.*" —Dt 4:1-6

But God

In matters of law, *proximate cause* is an event or condition related to the circumstances of injury that is held to be the cause of that injury. To prove cause, a test is used. It is the "*but for*" test. For example, *but for* the debris strewn on the sidewalk, the injured party would not have tripped and sustained a fall.

I had an uncle from Italy who owned an Italian deli. He aged huge provolone cheeses in the basement and lived in fear of mice eating his expensive cheese. Because of this anxiety, he kept cats around the deli to solve the problem. One day he found a cat sitting on his slicing machine. Miraculously, although he was an easily agitated man, he nonetheless maintained his composure, and didn't kill the cat. In a defeated and resigned tone of voice he explained this restraint in his heavily accented broken English: "If it were no for de cheese!" That was his way of saying *but for* the need to protect his cheese from the many mice, he would have killed that cat. I love that story.

In God's word, I read of this *but for* concept. It is at the very heart of the Gospel. It is used frequently by Paul in his epistles. For example, in Ephesians 2, Paul explains that we were all dead in our transgressions and sin, in times past, and followed only the lusts of our flesh—

> "Among them we too all formerly lived in the lusts of our flesh, indulging the desires of the flesh and of the mind, and were by nature children of wrath, even as the rest.
>
> *But God*, being rich in mercy, because of His great love with which He loved us, even when we were dead in our transgressions, made us alive together with Christ; by grace you have been saved..." Eph 2:3-5 (NASB)

But God! Do you see that? *But for* His great love toward us, and His richness of mercy, we would *still* be dead and separated from God. Again,—

> "Herein is love, not that we loved God, *but that He* loved us (first), and sent His Son to be the propitiation for our sins. Beloved, if God loved us so, we ought also to love one another."

No! It is not that we loved God!— *but for* God loving us first and sending His son to be a satisfaction for our sin that we are saved!

> "*But God* commanded His love toward us, in that while we were yet sinners, Christ died for us." —Rm 5:8

> "Not by works of righteousness which we have done, *but (God)* according to His mercy,— saved us." —Ti 3:5

> "*But...God* be thanked, whereas you were servants of sin, you have obeyed from the heart that system of teaching in which you have been instructed." —Rm 6:17

Can we just stop here and praise the Lord?

In 1 Corinthians 1:27, Paul is appealing to the condition of the congregation, in that they were neither mighty nor noble. He said; "*But God* hath chosen the foolish things of the world to confound the wise, and God hath chosen the weak things of the world to confound the things which are mighty." He goes on to say that no flesh should glory as this salvation is not of themselves. "*But of Him* are ye in Christ Jesus, who of God is made unto us wisdom and righteousness and sanctification and redemption. That as it is written, He that glorieth, let him glory in the Lord." You see, all that believers are and have, they owe entirely to God, and all the riches of salvation reside in Christ. Righteousness, a concept with legal dimensions, was credited to our account because of what Jesus did. He that began the good work continually sanctifies us, all thanks to His atonement.

Paul goes on to explain about the wisdom of God that was revealed to us: "*But God* hath revealed them unto us by His Spirit." He explains that he and Apollos planted and watered, "*But God* gave the increase." In our temptations Paul explains: "*But God* is faithful, who will not suffer you to be tempted above that ye are able." God has planned it so there be no divisions in his body, "*But God* hath tempered the body together (made different elements one) having given more abundant honor to that part which lacked." God is instrumental even in our resurrected body. "*But God* giveth it a body as it hath pleased Him."

When Paul declares:

> "*But by* the grace of God I am what I am", he is telling us all about the mercy, love and grace of our Savior, who did it all, and but for him we can do nothing. Paul also shows how he obeyed from the heart given to him— "His grace which was bestowed upon me was not in vain, but I labored more abundantly than they all, yet not I, *but by* the grace of God which was with me."

We stand and act, not in the wisdom of men, but in the power of God. We can know this wisdom and power if we have the mind of Christ.

So who gets the glory? Who did it? What was the cause of our salvation? Who gave us a new song and a heart of flesh and the wisdom of God? Who did that?

My uncle would have said: "If it were no for Christ!"
Can we all say Amen?

Know Doctrine
Know Division

You may have seen the bumper sticker—

NO CHRIST - NO LOVE
KNOW CHRIST - KNOW LOVE

Please let me introduce you to another that has helped me in my Christian walk—

NO DOCTRINE - NO DIVISION
KNOW DOCTRINE - KNOW DIVISION

A bumper sticker sent from God.

Proverbs 4 commands:

"Hear, ye children, the instruction of a Father, and *attend to know understanding*. For *I give you good doctrine*, forsake ye not *my law.*" Prv 4:1-2

And we know that—

"Where there is *no vision, the people perish*; but he that keepeth the law, happy is he." —Prv 29:18

Do you see how God in Proverbs equates his law with good doctrine and that those that keep his law are contrasted with those who are perishing from a lack of vision. So, yes, it could be said that with no doctrine there is no division but with no doctrine there is also no truth, no church and no vision, and so His people perish.

I see a church today that frightens me to death. It is a church that has lost its vision; a nation not aware that it is at war. A church too quick to seek peace at the sacrifice of truth, in a rush for some ecumenical unity, having no direction, discernment, or distinction, while open to deception and demons. Many are on a self-directed path of temporal happiness, unable to be delivered from "the way of the evil man, from the man that speaketh perverse things."

Our loving God has not left us without direction or knowledge of the path we must take. "In the way of righteousness is life; and in the pathway thereof there is no death." Remember that peace and love should rule in the life of a child of God. He asks us to, "apply our hearts unto instruction, and thine ears to the words of knowledge." Instruction from the Lord and the knowledge that He has revealed in scripture is the *good doctrine* that he has given for our safety and blessing.

Follow my thoughts, and trust me on this. You may presently be on a self-directed, self-destructive path. If indeed you have been saved then you must remember that with that God given salvation you have given up trying to save yourself,— trusting completely in the work of Christ. You have trusted God for your eternal future; so in living daily,—do the same thing. Lean not on your own understanding or on the strength of your own right arm. Proverbs 3 says: "Be not wise in thine own eyes: fear the Lord, and depart from evil." He that began the good work in you will also direct your path. But how are we to live? Which way do we go? How do we gain the faith to do it all? Saints, please let the Spirit do His work in you.

God says we must have His law written on our hearts. He also told us we need the foreskin of our hearts circumcised. Can you do these things? Certainly not! But what is impossible for man to do is always possible for God. Seek His word with all your heart. Learn all you can. Then wait on the Lord and He will direct your ways. Trust and pray remembering that without Him you can do nothing. You also need to seek His will. So then, what should be your posture and prayer? Beg, cry out, storm the gates of heaven with prayer, and claim the promises. Know your God. Know His word. Seek Him as the best love of your life, this requires that you *come out of yourself* in the sense that George Whitefield, wrote:

> "I know Christ is all in all. Man is nothing. He hath a free will to go to hell, but none to go to heaven, 'til God worketh in him to will and to do His good pleasure. Oh the excellency of the doctrine of election and of the saint's final perseverance. I am persuaded, 'til a man comes to believe and feel these important truths, he cannot *come out of himself*, but when convinced of these and assured of their application to his own heart, he then walks by faith indeed."

Can we agree that this must apply to our whole walk and sanctification? That we are blind and helpless without the light to our path? Please trust me when I say that I have found God's word to be absolutely true. Mankind has no answers, only a way that seems right, directed by pride and a quest for comfort. Our willful violation of conscience contains within itself the seed of destruction. Don't hinder the work of God in your conscience. Test everything against the clear doctrines of the Bible. Is it lawful, expedient? Clearly so? How do we know? The safe sure course of God's Word is always preferred. You've got to know, to go.

Proverbs 1:33 says: "But whosoever hearkeneth unto me shall dwell safely, and shall be quiet from fear of evil." Know the truth that frees you from your own headship and sin. Doctrine is essential to live, serve, and love. "No good thing will He withhold from them that walk uprightly." (Ps 84:11)

More from Whitefield explaining proper doctrine—

"If I had a voice so great, and could speak so loud, as that the whole world could hear me, I would cry, "Be not righteous over-much," by bringing your righteousness to Christ, and by being righteous in your own eyes. Man must be abased, that God may be exalted.

The *imputed righteousness** of Jesus Christ is a comfortable doctrine to all real Christians; and you sinners, who ask what you must do to be saved? How uncomfortable would it be, to tell you by good works, when, perhaps, you have never done one good work in all your life: this would be driving you to despair, indeed: no; "Believe in the Lord Jesus Christ, and you shall be saved:" therefore none of you need go away despairing. Come to the Lord Jesus by faith, and he shall receive you. You have no righteousness of your own to depend on. If you are saved, it is by the righteousness of Christ, through his atonement, his making a sacrifice for sin: his righteousness must be imputed to you, otherwise you cannot be saved."

---

*Imputed righteousness is the teaching in Scripture explaining that— although the one putting his faith in Christ for the forgiveness of his/her sins continues to commit sin they are nonetheless considered righteous (sinless) because the sinlessness of Christ is treated by God as if it were theirs. Christ's record of perfect obedience to the law in everything is reckoned to the sinner who puts their faith in Him. God the father looks at the sinner as if he were His spotless Son. In Scripture this concept is illustrated by such descriptions as the sinner being "clothed" in the white and spotless robe of Christ. This robe is symbolic of the righteousness of Jesus imputed (reckoned) to the sinner through faith.

Have Thy Way, O Lord

Have you ever been struck by how little we actually know about what lies before us;— how uncertain life is? How can we best pick our way through the confusing future that lies ahead?

The prophet wrote:

Thus saith the LORD, Stand ye in the ways, and see, and ask for the old paths, where is the good way, and walk therein, and ye shall find rest for your souls. —Jer 6:16

So we can be confident that in the midst of a life that is often bewildering and challenging there is always "the good way" and "the old paths" that we can confidently walk in and find rest, even for our very souls.

In my preparation for this devotion I came upon a book entitled *Between the Lights*. It was written in 1888, and the author, quotes Ephraim Peabody who expresses some of the thoughts I've had, but says it so much better than I would.

He writes:

"One thing is certain, that if you desire improvement in anything, it will never come to you accidentally. It must begin in a distinct, resolved purpose to make a change for the better.

I call on you to give this day to a serious review of your life, of what you have been living for, and of what you purpose henceforth to live for. Let it be today and begin aright. Here you stand at the parting of the ways: some road you are to take; and as you stand here, consider and know how it is that you intend to live. Carry no bad habits, no corrupting associations, no enmities and strifes, into this new year. Leave these behind, and let the dead past bury it's dead; leave them behind, and thank God that you are able to leave them".

I love J.R. Miller's thoughts on the right balance to strike between that which has past and the future we must face:

"It is never wise to live in the past. There are indeed some uses of our past which are helpful, and which bring blessing. We should remember our past lost condition to keep us humble and faithful. We should remember past failures and mistakes, that we may not repeat them. We should remember past mercies, that we may have confidence in new needs or trails in the future. We should remember past comforts, that there may be stars in our sky when night comes again. But while there are true uses of memory, we should guard against living in the past. We should draw our life's inspirations not from memory, but from hope; not from what is gone, but from what is yet to come. Forgetting the things which are behind, we should reach forward unto those things which are before."

Horatius Bonar wrote a great poem entitled *Thy Way, O Lord* in which he contemplates the way set before him:

"Thy way, not mine, O Lord, However dark it be! Lead me by Thine own hand; Choose out the path for me.

Smooth let it be or rough, It will be still the best; Winding or straight it matters not, It leads me to Thy rest.

I dare not choose my lot, I would not if I might; Choose Thou for me, my God, So shall I walk aright.

The kingdom that I seek is thine; so let the way that leads to it be Thine, else I must surely stray.

Not mine, not mine the choice in things or great or small; be Thou my guide, my strength, my wisdom, and my all."

Saints, we are each individually (and as a church body) heading on a path, the details of which we know not, but with the help of God, we can have confidence that we can consistently move from darkness into greater light. Let's use the Word and the strength of the Lord to do right, where once we did wrong.

"Eyes that look, are common. Eyes that see, are rare."
—Oswald Chambers

"But the path of the just is as the shining light, that shineth more and more unto the perfect day." —Prv 4:18

To be given light obligates us to follow it. To see duty, requires that we do it. Follow the light to everlasting day and the One that loves us with everlasting love. At the crossroads, look to God's road map, ask for the way while on your knees so that you'll be heard. You'll know the road by it's narrowness—walk in it and enjoy it's promised rest.

Deliver Me?

God harden me against myself,
This coward with pathetic voice
Who craves for ease and rest and joys
Myself, arch-traitor to myself;
My hollowest friend, my deadliest foe,
My clog whatever road I go.
Yet One there is can curb myself,
Can roll the strangling load from me
Break off the yoke and set me free.

—Christina Georgina Rossetti (1830-1894)

What Does Christmas Mean to Me?

Come with me into the word of God to explore the meaning of Christmas. The word Christmas is actually a contraction of "Christ's mass"—the celebration of the Messiah. It brings those of us who love Him great joy along with so great a salvation. It is the gospel personified. "And the word was made flesh, and dwelt among us, and we beheld His glory." —John 1:14

Let us test this truth by the word. In Luke's gospel we read,

"And there were in the same country, shepherds abiding in the field, keeping watch over their flock by night. And, lo, the angel of the Lord came upon them, and the glory of the Lord shone round about them: and they were sore afraid. And the angel said to them, Fear not: for behold, I bring you *good tidings* of *great joy*, which shall be to all people. For *unto you* is born this day in the city of David *a Savior*, which is Christ the Lord." —Luke 2:8

The angel said "I bring you good tidings", the good tidings was the good news, or the gospel, which was the glorious news that "unto us a Savior is born" and great joy accompanies it. This phrase "great joy" is used in only three places in the Bible, but they are notable:

1. At Christ's birth. (Matt. 2: 9-11)
2. At His resurrection. (Matt. 28: 7-9)
3. At Christ's ascension. Luke 24: 51-53

The kind of joy described in 1 Peter pertains to Christians kept by the power of God through faith unto salvation—

> "Whom having not seen, ye love, in whom, though now you see Him not, yet believing, ye rejoice with *joy* unspeakable and full of glory; receiving the end of your faith, even the *salvation* of your souls." —1 Pt 1:8

The book of Luke begins by announcing "great joy", and ends with the disciples filled with great joy receiving the end of their faith,—the salvation of their souls.

The Christmas message *is* the gospel—

> **"For unto us a child is born, unto us a son is given: and the government shall be upon His shoulder: and His name shall be called Wonderful, Counselor, The Mighty God, The Everlasting Father, The Prince of Peace."** —Isaiah 9:6

"For unto us a child is born..."

> "Behold, a virgin shall be with child, and shall bring forth a son, and they shall call his name Emmanuel, which being interpreted is, God with us."

"A Son is given..."

We need only go to John's the gospel:

> "For God so loved the world, that he gave his only begotten Son, that whosoever believeth in him should not perish, but have everlasting life". —Jn 3:16

John says more in 1 John:

> "And this is the record, that God hath given to us eternal

life, and this is in His Son". —1 John 5:11

"And the government shall be upon His shoulder"... Isa 9:7

"Of the increase of his government and peace there shall be no end, upon the throne of David, and upon his kingdom, to order it, and establish it with judgment and with justice from henceforth even forever. The zeal of the LORD of hosts will perform this". (Young's literal translation states it clearer: "And the princely power is on his shoulder. And he doth call his name".)

"Wonderful..."

"Your statutes are wonderful; therefore I obey them." —Ps 119

"Counselor..." Ps 119:24

Your statutes are my delight; they are my counselors. Wonderful and Counselor describe the word of God, which is the power of God unto salvation. Revelation describes the Word in v. 21:5 as "true and faithful". And again in Rev 19:11 Jesus on His white horse is called: "faithful and true". (v. 13) His name is called the Word of God.

"Mighty God..."

"The LORD your God is with you, he is MIGHTY to save".
—Zephaniah 3:17

"Everlasting..."

The bible speaks of his salvation as everlasting. Isa 45:17 "But Israel will be saved in the Lord with an everlasting salvation: ye shall not be ashamed nor confounded world without end". Jer 32:40 "and I will make an everlasting covenant with them, that I will not turn away from them, to do them good; but I will put my fear in their hearts, that they shall not depart from me". He gives everlasting life and speaks of an everlasting gospel or good tidings. Jn 5:24 and Rev 14:6

"Prince of Peace..."

"The Lord will give strength unto His people; the Lord will bless his people with Peace". —Ps 29:11

"For he is our peace, who hath made both one, and hath broken down the middle wall of partition between us." —Eph 2:14

"There is no peace, saith the Lord, unto the wicked" —Isa 49:22

"I will hear what God the Lord will speak: for he will speak peace unto his people, and to his saints". —Ps 85:8

Could the good news be any clearer as it shines through the Christmas verses of both the Old and New testaments? There lay in this babe, the origin of our righteousness, and the beginning of man's redemption. This child who is the Mighty Jehovah, with everlasting rule over eternal life given to His people with great joy set before Him. A true God-man wonder showing the character of Emmanuel. This obscure figure of Emmanuel is brought to clear light. We now know of his kingdom, throne, world rule, peaceful reign, and eternal kingdom, as well as His virgin birth. More than this, we see God incarnate, the Gospel of Christmas.

So then what should and does Christmas mean to me? Everything: A gift from a gracious Father to have us know the joy and love of His Son. Everything of eternal worth, everything cherished, love beyond description, a work that began and ended humbly but more meaningful and life changing than any other event in history.

This year, see the gospel declared by His birth and celebrate the Messiah.

For *unto us* a child is born.

Christmas Peace

Although the Christmas day has come
'midst scenes of rush and hurry,
there is a place of quiet calm—
a refuge from all worry.
it's found by harking back to One,
Who, in a manger laid,
Was born to die that men might live;
the One by whom all men were made.
He takes our anxious fears away,
our guilty minds are freed
when we but look in humble faith
to His atoning deed:
the blood, the sweat, the grief, the gore,
the anguished cry of pain,
all whisper, "Peace!, the storm is o'er,
My loss is now your gain!"
So, rest beneath a Christmas tree,
but rest yourself e'en more
beneath the tree where Jesus hung
until the storm was o'er.

—Anthony Rotolo 12/24/97

The Sin Unto Death

I wrote the following letter to a friend that was struggling with understanding 1 John 5:16,17 and asked for my opinion on it:

Hi Mike,

You asked for understanding on 1 John 5:16,17, I hope this helps.

> "If any man see his brother sin a sin which is not unto death, he shall ask, and he shall give him life for them that sin not unto death. there is a sin unto death: I do not say that he shall pray for it. All unrighteousness is sin; and there is a sin not unto death." —1 Jn 5:16,17

First of all we know that *all* sin is ultimately unto death, that is, *any* sin. James 2:10 explains; "For whosoever shall keep the whole law, and yet offend in one point, (just one sin) he is guilty of all (not every sin but of breaking the law as a coherent whole)."

1 John 3:4 teaches that *any* sin is a transgression of the law.

> "Now we know that what things soever the law saith, it saith to them who are under the law: that every mouth may be stopped, and all the world may become guilty before God."
> —Rm 3:19

"...for the wages of sin is death." —Rm 6:23

So any sin produces spiritual death, and the whole world is guilty. "But the gift of God is eternal life through Jesus Christ our Lord." (Rom 6:23)

Secondly, there is one sin described in Scripture as the sin that cannot be pardoned— "the sin unto death", (which is to say *eternal* death in hell). This sin is also called the "blasphemy of the Holy Spirit" which is attributing to Satan, what is clearly the work of the Holy Spirit. Please see; Mt 12:32, Mk 3:29, Lk 12:10.

Thirdly, so we can then confidently say that a sin that is "not unto death" would be every other sin a man could possibly commit, as all manner of sins besides blasphemy of the Holy Spirit explained above, can be forgiven by God in Christ.

> "But now being made free from sin, and becoming servants to God, ye have your fruit unto holiness, and the end, everlasting life." —Rm 6:22

I believe the death spoken of in 1 Jn 5:16 is eternal death, or hell, and that vs. 16 is speaking to fellow believers or brothers. Our prayers should always include the needs of our fellow Saints, and so if you see a brother or sister sin a sin, other than the one unto death, you ask, and God shall give life to them that sin not unto death. We pray also for the lost, that God do the saving.

> "And this is the confidence that we have in him, that, if we ask anything according to his will, he heareth us: and if we know that he hear us, whatsoever we ask, we know that we have the petitions that we desired of him." —1 Jn 5:14,15

Truly, we are to pray with confidence for all, that God grant eternal life. Job's prayers were accepted by the Lord for his friends (Job 42:7-10). Read about the intercession of Moses in Psalm 106:21.

> "...and the prayer of faith shall save the sick, and the Lord shall raise him up, and *if he have committed sins, they shall be forgiven him.* —Jas 5:15

"...the effectual fervent prayer of a righteous man availeth much. —Jas 5:16b

Continue reading until v. 20:

"He which converteth the sinner from the error of his way, shall save a soul from death." —Jas 5:20

God will work through sinners saved by grace praying for other sinners,— that they may be saved.

I hope this humble explanation helps you gain some insight into this passage, and I hope you'll benefit by a similar sentiment from the great old saint and fellow sinner Matthew Henry:

"We ought to pray for others, as well as ourselves. There are sins that war against spiritual life in the soul, and the life above. We cannot pray that the sins of the impenitent and unbelieving should, while they are such, be forgiven them; or that mercy, which supposes the forgiveness of sins, should be granted them, while they wilfully continue such. But we may pray for their repentance, for their being enriched with faith in Christ, and thereupon for all other saving mercies. We should beseech the Lord to pardon and recover the fallen, as well as to relieve the tempted and afflicted. And let us be truly thankful that no sin, of which any one truly repents, is unto death."

Prayer

Being recently convicted by a great sermon, I vowed to do something to improve my often neglected prayer life. I thought I should pray about it. I needed to reflect on it's purpose and the impact sincere and fervent prayer should have on my life.

Spurgeon reminds us that Peter urgently prayed:

"Lord save me!" —Matthew 14:30.

Peter's was an immediate plea, not waiting for an appointed time in a prayer closet, the kind of reliance and continuous recognition of needed help we must have in this world. Spurgeon encourages us to cultivate prayer, making it a habit, being direct, and covering our needs. Peter's prayer was effectual, as the Lord did save him. "Where'er we seek Him, He is found, and every place we seek Him is hallowed ground." (Spurgeon)

Prayerless souls are Christ-less souls and graceless souls, Spurgeon warns, and the criticism of Job— "Thou....restrainest prayer before God", should not be ours.

Peter's prayer was a supplication or a petition type of prayer. While his was sober and led by the Holy Spirit, how often do we approach God with a: "God, I need something so I'm asking..." type of prayer. How often are our requests of God made selfishly and without regard for His glory?

Years ago I was taught an acronym that has proved enormously helpful to me. It serves to shape my prayers in a way that is more glorifying to God. So as I pray I remember the word ACTS:

> **A**...............**A**doration
> **C**...............**C**onfession
> **T**...............**T**hanksgiving
> **S**...............**S**upplication

Please consider the order, and how supplication comes after first giving worship and honor to so great a God, remembering and confessing our sins against Him, and giving thanks for all we have already been given, for "What do you have that you weren't given?"

Mary knew how to pray: "My soul doth magnify the Lord, and my spirit hath rejoiced on God my Savior. For He hath regarded the low estate of His handmaiden...He is mighty...done great things... holy is His name." On and on, Mary praises God in the past tense, proclaiming: "He hath shewed strength, scattered the proud, put down the mighty, filled the hungry, helped Israel." "And his mercy is on them that fear Him from generation to generation."

Mary was concerned only with praise, adoration and thanksgiving after receiving so great an honor and blessing. We can well imagine her prayers of supplication while watching her son carry the cross to Calvary.

In professing my adoration of God in prayer, recognizing my trespasses, and acknowledging His gracious provision, I am less inclined to ask for those things I merely want in order to gratify my flesh. I learn to be content with the countless blessings that God has already provided.

Do you remember the account in the Garden— "And the Lord God called to Adam, and said unto him, 'Where art thou?'" You see, at that point Adam had fallen by disobeying God and was already experiencing a taste of what separation from God feels like. Where are you? Are you experiencing communion with the Lord as He would have? Are you avoiding God? (As if that were possible.) Are you regularly confessing your sins to the Lord?

Once I asked a fellow saint whose walk with the Lord I admired: "You must have very little to confess." His answer surprised me as he explained: "The closer you come to the light, the clearer you see your sin." We must understand just how fallen we are.

When writing about prayer, the famous author of a *Pilgrim's Progress*, John Bunyan explained:

> "Prayer is a sincere, sensible, affectionate pouring out of the heart or soul to God, through Christ, in the strength and assistance of the Holy Spirit, for such things as God has promised, or according to His Word, for the good of the church, with submission in faith to the will of God."

Spurgeon wrote:

> "We must fight as well as pray. Though effort without prayer would be presumption, prayer without effort is mockery."

I love the pithy saying:

> "Pray as if works don't count. Work as if prayers don't count."

As God's people, we are to be the first Bible that people "read", and our life should preach a sermon all the time. Yes, I know that while still in the flesh I will fail. I will need to continually confess my sins and keep coming to God for help, but with that help, I will have less to confess, and will more faithfully seek His will.

"Hearken unto the voice of my cry, my king and my God: for unto thee will I pray." —Ps 5:2

Walking in the Light

"Hurry Vin, we're late for the movie! my wife Rosemary said as we rushed into a totally dark theater. "Hey!", yells a man whose eye I just poked while groping in the dark. "Rose! Let's just stand still here until we get used to the dark." (Good thing I did as she would have momentarily sat on an old lady.)

I share this embarrassing story because I want to explore the question "What fellowship does light have with darkness?"

When the Apostle John contrasts light with dark, we begin to understand how really dark our world is. We are exhorted in Scripture, as "children of the light" to have no fellowship with darkness, to walk away from it and reprove it. Unfortunately, too many are standing still and getting used to the dark.

One pastor recently pointed out how we get used to the darkness by listing the ways we compromise, euphemize, and reduce what the Bible calls sin to acceptable behavior:

Drunkenness becomes "under the influence."

Murder becomes "temporary insanity."

Abortion becomes "free choice."

Same-sex marriage becomes "an alternate lifestyle."

How can we learn how to live as we should working out our salvation with fear and trembling while pleasing our Lord? How do we cease doing what is done in the dark or approving of it? How do we not destroy our soul through our own stupidity?

The Puritan Robert Bolton writes:

> "It is the only right everlasting method to turn men from darkness to light, from the power of Satan unto God; First, is to wound by the law, and then to heal by the gospel...We must be sensible of our spiritual blindness."

Did you get that—Wound by the law—Heal by the gospel.

One of the main purposes of the law is to wound our hearts. As we meditate upon God's law we see how far short we come of the perfect standard of righteousness. It should grieve us and wound us in our spirit. Only by this work of the law will we be prepared properly for the good news of the healing gospel.

Why do we participate in the darkness of this world? Why do we not esteem God's perfect law? The Bible declares "male and female He created them." (Gn 5:2) and "man cleaves to a wife, one flesh that lives as one." (Mt 19:5) and again, "every man had his own wife, and every wife, her own husband." (1 Cor 7:2) but we sit silently by while the marriage institution is attacked and eroded on all sides. We give no warning to those who continue in various sins born out of contempt for marriage.

How about drunkenness? Ephesians 5:18 warns us "do not take in excess", and 1 Corinthians 6:12: "don't be brought under the power of anything", and yet how many of us while perhaps not getting drunk with alcohol nonetheless get "drunk" from allowing some other excess to control our lives? Food, drugs, anger, etc.

The bottom line is this: We don't want to be a splash in the lake of fire, nor see others cast into it. We must walk in the light as God gives us the light. Be wounded by His Law, but healed by His saving grace. You see while the Law has a proper place in first wounding us, the glorious gospel of Christ which proclaims that Jesus earned us a place in Heaven comes and heals. That is if indeed we accept that it is by Christ's work of redemption alone that we may be saved. The healing balm of the gospel says Christ will heal the wounds of your sin by His atoning work. When we repent of our sin and accept His sacrifice on our behalf we are healed.

Recognize what is darkness. Own your sin. Confess it. Learn the truth and the way. Pray always for help, intercession, and guidance from the Lord. You have already been given the ability, and are without excuse if you remain in the dark and not in the light given us by our Lord, Creator and Savior.

The joy that comes with this great salvation is that the Law will take on a new perspective. While it will always wound our conscience if we transgress it, it can become a blessed servant to a life of righteousness and good conscience. When we understand that the law has the added purpose of protecting us from harm we can appreciate it as it illuminates the way before us.

In times past, a servant would walk ahead of his master with candles attached to his feet, so that the path was lit. The book of Psalms tells us that God's word is that lamp to our feet and that light to our path. The Psalmist extols: "Oh, how I love your law! I meditate upon it all day long!" (Ps 119:97) Our path is the life we are living and only by delighting in God's law can we see (understand) our way upon that path.

> "Enter not into the path of the wicked, and go not in the way of evil men. Avoid it, pass not by it, turn from it, and pass away. For they sleep not, except they have done mischief; and their sleep is taken away, unless they cause some to fall. For they eat the bread of wickedness, and drink the wine of violence. But the path of the just is as the shining *light*, that

shineth more and more unto the perfect day. The way of the wicked is as *darkness*: they know not at what they stumble. My son, attend to my words; incline thine ear unto my sayings. Let them not depart from thine eyes; keep them in the midst of thine heart. For they are life unto those that find them, and health to all their flesh." —Prv 4:14-22

Where is God When I'm in Pain?

Do you ever ask why must we need to suffer? My friend Pastor Gabriel Otero answered that question in a recent sermon. He likens our pain to that of receiving an inoculation— a little pain endured presently to accomplish a much greater good later.

In James 5:10 we are told to take the example of the prophets who suffered and endured. Jeremiah wound up in jail, but wrote Lamentations because of that suffering, and requested of God, that He "Turn thou us unto thee, O LORD, and we shall be turned; renew our days as of old". (Lam 5:21)

Isaiah wanted to quit, but God asked him to be faithful and gave him the strength to persevere. Paul reminds us to glory in our tribulation, as it works in us: patience, experience, and hope. These trials give us hope as we become more like Jesus.

When we experience the kind of pain that will never be forgotten this side of the grave, He is with us in the midst of it, and is afflicted with us. He knows our pain. See Isa 63:9:

> "In all their affliction he was afflicted, and the angel of his presence saved them: in his love and in his pity he redeemed them; and he bare them, and carried them all the days of old."

We may complain in pain, but God is with us. We don't understand now, this side of heaven, but God is making it better for them that are called according to His purpose (Romans 8:28).

> "For unto you it is given in behalf of Christ, not only to believe on Him, but also to suffer for His sake." —Phil 1:29

Only through His grace are we able to do that. He gifted us with understanding the gospel and believing, but it was also gifted us to suffer.

> "For I reckon that the sufferings of this present time are not worthy to be compared with the glory which shall be revealed in us." —Rom 8:18

Walk by faith, not sight. God may not minimize our sufferings, but they will magnify the promises to come. Express your suffering, but do not complain. What we do with our difficulties is what matters. Not what happened, but what we do through it and with it. He provides our strength and help. Our pain will be there, but so is His help.

> "And as Jesus passed by, he saw a man which was blind from his birth. And his disciples asked him saying, Master, who did sin, this man, or his parents, that he was born blind? Jesus answered, Neither hath this man sinned, nor his parents: but that the works of God should be made manifest in him." —Jn 9:1

Please don't add unnecessary suffering to your pain by assuming that you are being punished for your sins. Yes, it's healthy to consider whether a trial could be a chastening from God if we can see a connection between a habitually sinful behavior or situation that we have not turned from and our present suffering but that is certainly not always the case. Job was a righteous man and lived uprightly and yet it pleased the Lord to bring terribly painful trials to his life for no reasons pertaining to a failure on Job's part. Just remember: He knows why, and you may never know fully, until glory. What you must trust is His Word that commands us:

> "Fear thou not; for I am with thee; be not dismayed; for I am your God: I will strengthen thee; yea, I will help thee; yea, I will uphold thee with the right hand of my righteousness."
> —2 Tim 1:17

Where is God in your pain? Where is the help you need? He never went anywhere. He is right there with you in the middle of it all. Trust, obey, and glorify Him. He is equipping us and bringing us closer to Him. Don't question why, as if there is some unfairness with God, but seek new insight, direction, grace and help. We need to learn, grow in grace, not question His goodness, and continue to pray.

Recently, I heard a story about a Grandma baking a cake with her grandchild. The child wanted to taste everything immediately, and wouldn't wait for the batter to be complete and the cake baked in the oven. He gagged on the raw eggs, coughed on the dry flour, spit out the oil and equally decried all the individual ingredients. Finally, though, in the fullness of time, the cake was fully baked, cooled and decorated.

It was delicious.

Our hurts and trials in this life are very much like the separate ingredients of the cake. As they come, they are distasteful and we can't imagine anything beautiful and delightful culminating from the mixture of all these hurts. We certainly don't understand them all working for good in our lives but God does and is with us at all times in our suffering.

There was a deep, dark, horrible Friday for our Lord, but He endured it for the joy He understood would follow. Many of us are experiencing our worst fears and hurts right now. But then there came that beautiful Sunday morning which blessed us all. Believe and have faith— your Sunday will come.

One Step At A Time

In the gospel of Mark (v. 8:33) Jesus rebukes Peter, calls him Satan, and accuses him of being mindful of earthly things? Then He speaks plainly, explaining that they must take up their cross and deny themselves as they follow Him.

I don't know about you, but to me, the commands of Jesus can be terrifying. The cross Jesus demands that we take up, requires us to give up our world and its comforts, and to serve others before ourselves. We are to called to— Be holy, for He is holy, study to show ourselves approved, husbands to love their wives as Christ loved His church, and wives to submit to their husbands, children to obey their parents.

Surely this can't be true, not in "this world"... not in a world ruled by Satan, where our greatest idol is ourselves, where women are warned not to ultimately trust their husband but to have a career to provide for themselves, to have an escape plan,... where children can't submit because they've never seen an example of submission... where men can't model headship because they don't understand what loving headship is.

Please help me! Did Jesus not say— that all things are possible if we believe? Does the Spirit still testify of, and glorify Christ? Can we still do all things through Christ who strengthens us? Is it still true, that whatsoever is of God overcomes the world?

May I submit that the flute has been piped for us all, and we have not danced. We have been mourned to, but have not wept. Let me add myself, a redeemed saint, cleansed by the blood of my Savior, and filled with His Spirit, right there at the top of the list— Yes, I have not wept or danced *as faithfully as I should have,*... but, I am persuaded that if I can do nothing without Him, then it must be equally true that I can do all things, *with him.*

Obedience can be a daunting prospect. It is all but impossible without the help of the Spirit. It requires our reliance upon Him. I, for one, pledge to start immediately, one small step at a time, to seek and serve My God, my wife and my children. When *what I want*, screams for attention I will ask that God give me the grace to put others before myself. I will trust that as I seek Him, He will give me the desires of my heart. What about you?

If you've been lacking time with your children, will you give them an extra half an hour? Will you start today with small steps? If you need more intimacy in your marriage, will you begin by simply holding hands? We must persevere with small, positive, obtainable steps. As we see the blessings from what small but concerted efforts yield we will derive the encouragement we need. As we discipline ourselves to be more faithful we can re-evaluate our failures, they cannot be permanent. Humbled by self-examination and confession, I will please my God who wants me to experience this life more abundantly. I will trust as a child even if that means taking small, even baby steps in obedience.

Recognize your God-given power to overcome! Satan is no longer our master! We are free indeed, free to ask anything in His name, and in His will, knowing it will be answered. We are not only separated to Him, but exalted...

> "And I heard a voice from heaven saying, Come out of her my people, that ye be not partakers of her sins, and that ye receive not of her plagues. For her sins have reached unto heaven..."

I want my future deeds not to reach unto heaven because of their sinful character, but to be stored there as treasure.

No one knows better than we do, that when we forsake others, and serve ourselves with short-sighted pleasures, we deny the gift given us from God. Take small steps in bowing the knee to obedient submission. The devil hates submission. He also loves to destroy marriages. How evil it is to whisper in the ears of wives that when they submit, they are not equal. God tells us otherwise. He tells us that in Christ we all have equal worth and dignity but that when a wife submits to the loving headship of her husband she glorifies God and strengthens the family as well as the church. Make those small steps wives.

Husbands, what small steps must you take? You are called to lead in your home by example. To lovingly consider your wife as you would your own body. What small steps will you take to be more of a servant? Christ, our great example, no less than God His Father, was nonetheless subordinate to His Father in all things. Let us use God's formulas, for God's rewards. The world does not know God's plan for our families, but we do and we have the power to shine forth and magnify our Lord. Let's finally fill that hollow deep inside that cries for peace on earth and begin in our own households and church.

Brothers and sisters—

> "We are come unto Mount Sion, and unto the city of the living God, the heavenly Jerusalem, and to an innumerable company of angels... and to God the Judge of all, and to the spirits of *just men made perfect (complete).*" —Heb 12:22-23

Let us pledge to take whatever those small steps necessary toward growing into that mature "just man made complete" in Christ. One step at a time, abandon self, love and serve to the point where others say: "Show me your God!"

My "Never Again" List

I broke a heart today. It wasn't hard to do. I did it through a lack of patience, a harsh and uncontrolled outburst, and an angry abandonment of dignity. The immediate satisfaction of responding to what I deemed an irrational argument someone was having with me was not enough to soothe the remorse I felt later on. I broke a heart, and I grieved the Holy Spirit that requires I "be angry and sin not." And has told me time and again that "the anger of man does not work the righteousness of God." I said to myself: "Never Again!" Never again will I show so little love and patience, so much pride and anger. And so I started my "Never Again List."

Through the haunting feelings of disappointment, embarrassment and failure, the Holy Spirit worked through my conscience to identify the worldly technique, habit and pride I had justified myself in using. What could have been loving correction and instruction was lost in the volume of my rage. I know, that even when I feel assaulted by aggressive, even irrational behavior, I must remain humble and meek, all the while seeking the strength of my Savior and the instruction of His word, rather than to retaliate in my flesh. Never again.

I know it's good to acknowledge our failures, and not be callous to them. Ignoring our shortcomings and sinful habits will never promote growth in holiness. I thank God for the example of the apostle Paul, who cried: "O wretched man that I am! Who shall deliver me from the body of this death?" Thanks be to God that our deliverance and sanctification is from Him and that we are not left to our own devices. God forbid that we continue in the same sin, or ever forget that the burden of sin and our need of forgiveness was what first drove us to our knees, to Christ. I must always remember Paul's rhetorical question: "What fruit has been yielded by our sin?" —Rom 6:21

It seems to me, that no matter how hard we try, we continue to repeat hateful traits ingrained in us. We abandon social limits as we trash a dignity that should be treasured. All our intentions to show love, a good example, a godly persuasion, are blunted, even lost entirely, and not received by the one whose heart we might break in the bargain. When we resort to responding in our own strength and flesh we can offer no real solutions, nothing righteousness will result— we will only regret our retreat back to the world and it's methods. Many times it is the one closest to us, that we hurt the most. Never again!

So now I have my growing "Never Again" list. I've determined to never again lose patience, never again abandon a Spirit-controlled temperament, to never again jettison grace towards the other, and never again neglect prayer to God in the midst of a challenging interaction with another, especially those I hold nearest and dearest. Do I think that making a list is enough. Certainly not, but identifying where I need to grow is a start. Do I think I can keep this list and not do these same things again? That's biblically unrealistic. I'm a sinner, still in the flesh, so I will fall— but I won't use that as an excuse for my sin— only an excuse to rely more and more upon God. With His help I should see an improvement in these areas I lack.

We contribute nothing to our initial salvation, which is our justification, but we do cooperate with God in our growth in godliness, which is our sanctification. Once saved, we have a will that has been empowered by the Spirit and can choose to mortify the flesh and live for God. We can pray for help with our anger, our pride, and our flesh and Satan's influence upon us, and we can expect results. Selfishness, sloppiness, detachment, gossip and treacherous dealings can be replaced by love and loyalty. Pray that the Spirit instils in us: grace to others, thoughtful response and patience.

Saints, we can expect help from above with our "Never Again" list. I encourage you to begin yours today and seek God for your growth in holiness.

Praise God From Whom All Blessings Flow

I praise God that He has given us eyes to see His perfection and glory, and a heart to feel His love. I thank Him that my future is in His sovereign, omnipotent and omniscient hands, and that I am safe and have peace because He says that I do.

Do you know how many brothers and sisters still cannot rest in the promises and words of the Savior? They continue to rely on their own strength for their sanctification. How hopeless to think that we can bring something to God. He has it all already, and doesn't need what we might bring, since it would only be something He has made. The "already done" aspect of our salvation and future is really not appreciated enough, and that pagan lack of appreciation, diminishes what we can and must give— our thanks.

Some even believe they can lose the salvation secured for them by our Lord. When Jesus turned away unbelievers who were relying on the miracles they did in his name, He said: "I never knew you." Jesus didn't say "I knew you once but now I disown you." He never knew them or the impotent "god" they worshipped. I thank God daily that my salvation is not dependent on my sinful self. "It is the work of God that you believe on him who he has sent" "All that the Father giveth me shall come to me: and him that cometh to me I will no wise cast out."

Please see the plain truth expressed so well in a verse like Psalm 62:1,2:

> "My soul finds rest in God alone; my salvation comes from Him. He alone is my rock and my salvation; He is my fortress, I will never be shaken."

There will come a great shaking as described in Isa 2:19:

> "And they shall go into the holes of the rocks, and into the caves of the earth, for fear of the LORD, and for the glory of his majesty, when he ariseth to *shake* terribly the earth."

Thankfully those eternally secured in Christ can never be shaken out of the tree of life. "All which the Father hath given me I should lose nothing." —Jn 6:29,37,39.

It has all been done perfectly and completely by Jesus. Please understand how the effectual call works:

> "And we know that all things work together for good to them that love God, to them who are the *called* according to his purpose. For whom he *did* foreknow, he also *did* predestinate to be conformed to the image of his Son, that he might be the firstborn among many brethren. Moreover whom he did predestinate, them he also called: and whom he called, them he also justified: and whom he justified, them he also glorified." What shall we then say to these things? If God be for us, who can be against us? "Rm 8:28-31

Do you see how a right understanding of divine sovereignty gives great comfort? "Nothing can separate us from the love of God" —Rom 8:38 Nothing! "And who is he that will harm you, if ye be followers of that which is good." —1Pt 3:13 The fact that you are loved by the only one who counts, and are no longer separated by sin is the light that should shine brighter and brighter as you rest more and more in the peace that passeth all understanding.

Know your exalted position and let others see it. You should be the first Bible they ever see. Your joy, assurance and guaranteed hope is what they need to see.

John proclaims:

> "By this is love perfected with us, so that we may have confidence for the day of judgment, because as he is, so also are we in this world. There is no fear in love, but perfect love casts out fear. For fear has to do with punishment, and whoever fears has not been perfected in love. We love because he first loved us." 1 Jn 4:16-18

When you know you can never be shaken because you are in the Rock, love is perfected in you.

Our church motto is the Scripture verse: "To know Him and make Him known". You are truly a great witness when you know the sovereignty and accomplishment of God. When you believe the "already done" aspect of our salvation—

> "And from Jesus Christ, who is the faithful witness, and the first begotten of the dead, and the prince of the kings of the earth. Unto him that *loved* us, and *washed* us from our sins in His own blood, And hath *made us* kings and priests unto God and his Father; to him be glory and dominion for ever and ever. Amen." —Rev 1:5-6

Did you know you were a king? A priest? A prophet?, A co-heir with Christ? Well, He said it and I believe it. He did it all without my help, even if I don't understand every aspect of it, I still trust Him explicitly. I had as much to do with my spiritual birth, as I did with my physical birth. The difference is, in my first birth I was raised a sinner, and in my new birth, raised a king. Praise God, thank you Jesus!

> "O foolish Galatians, who hath bewitched you, that ye should not obey the truth, before whose eyes Jesus Christ hath been evidently set forth, crucified among you? This only would

I learn of you, Received ye the Spirit by the works of the law, or by the hearing of faith? Are ye so foolish? having begun in the Spirit, are ye now made perfect by the flesh?" —Gal 3:1-3

"Christ hath redeemed us from the curse of the law."
—Gal 3:13a

"You are all the children of God through faith in Jesus Christ."
—Gal 3:26

"And if ye be Christ's, then are ye Abraham's seed, and heirs according to the promise." —Gal 3:29

Do you truly believe you are Christ's? Then believe His word.

You have it all and no one can take it from you. That's the light you shine as you weep for those who do not love your Savior. But never be weary in well doing, knowing your brothers and sisters are out there also. You are required to be faithful, not successful. Only God knows when the kingdom comes to others, and who they are.

You can only proclaim what you know.

"I have set watchmen upon thy walls, O Jerusalem, which shall never hold their peace day nor night: ye that make mention of the Lord, keep not silence." —Isa 62:6

You children of Abraham who know Him, make Him known.

Woe Unto Me If I Do Not Preach The Gospel

In Romans, Paul touches upon the gift of prophecy—

"...whether prophecy, let us prophesy according to the proportion of faith." —Romans 12:6

The proportion of faith, means that what a prophet says, must be in harmony with what has already been spoken by God. The authority of the Word tests what is said.

When we say: "Thus saith the Lord" or, "I have a word from the Lord, " it had better be from the logos, the written revealed word. Our very faith is a reliance on the written word, and we must only speak that which is faithful.

God instructs us in Jeremiah 29:1-17. A false prophet named Hananiah speaks to Jeremiah in the house of the Lord. He claims there will be only 2 years of bondage, and then freedom. He is one who is giving a timeline, prophesying in the church, declaring peace, where there is none. Hananiah was a false prophet led by the spirit of error, and was deceived, a wandering star with no stability (in the greek: like a planet or star that is out of orbit).

The true prophet, Jeremiah had explained that all previous prophets had promised war and evil pestilence, pointing to an angry God. From Abel to Jeremiah the message was consistent, with every true prophet declaring that man was at war with God. God consistently preached judgment. The word of God cannot be broken, and will harmonize with no conflict.

In Jer 28:12-17 we see what becomes of a false prophet—

> Then the word of the LORD came unto Jeremiah the prophet, after Hananiah the prophet had broken the yoke from off the neck of the prophet Jeremiah, saying,
> "Go and tell Hananiah, saying, 'Thus says the LORD; You have broken the yokes of wood; but you shall make for them yokes of iron.
> For thus says the LORD of hosts, the God of Israel; I have put a yoke of iron upon the neck of all these nations, that they may serve Nebuchadnezzar king of Babylon; and they shall serve him: and I have given him the beasts of the field also.' "
> Then said the prophet Jeremiah unto Hananiah the prophet, "Hear now, Hananiah; The LORD has not sent you; but you make this people to trust in a lie."
> Therefore thus says the LORD; "Behold, I will cast you from off the face of the earth: this year you shall die, because you have taught rebellion against the LORD."
> So Hananiah the prophet died the same year in the seventh month.

God first declares that He is the Sovereign, in control of all (v. 14). He declares that He did not send Hananiah (v. 15). Then God gets him for preaching a lie that the people trusted in (v. 16).

> "Hearken not unto the words of the prophets that prophecy unto you: they make you vain: they speak a vision of their own heart, and not out of the mouth of the Lord." —Jer 23:16

Read 1 Timothy 3:2, see that elders are to be "apt to teach", they should demonstrate an aptitude to teach, responsible to know error and proclaim truth. God will test them and their obligation to expose the lie. (Dt 13:1-3) They must remove the false from their congregations. (Dt 13:9) Hananiah was killed. We are to kill the error, not fearing man, but fearing God and His Word.

"Beloved, believe not every spirit, but try the spirits whether they are of God; because many false prophets are gone out into the world." —1 Jn 4:1

"If any man teach otherwise, and consent not to wholesome words, even the words of our Lord Jesus Christ, and to the doctrine which is according to godliness; He is proud, knowing nothing, but doting about questions and strifes of words, whereof cometh envy, strife, railings, evil surmisings, perverse disputings of men of corrupt minds, and destitute of the truth, supposing that gain is godliness: from such withdraw thyself." —1 Tim 6:3-5

We can't say "Amen" *and* agree to the false, for if we do—

1. We undermine God's word,

2. We allow a lie,

3. We step out of bounds,— "If any man speak, let him speak the oracles of God,...that God in all things may be glorified through Jesus Christ, to whom be praise and dominion for ever and ever." —1 Pet. 4:11

4. Christ is not preached or exalted, as Christ *is* the whole counsel of God.

Jesus is the sum and substance of divine revelation. "Now faith is the substance (the person) of things hoped for, the evidence of things not seen." Heb. 11:1 Our faith must only rely on God's Word. We must insist upon hearing from Jesus, and about Jesus and glory in Him alone. We should be able to say: "I have seen the glory of God in Jesus."

From a NT commentary:

"The message of the people who prophesy should be in harmony with, or come forth out of the revealed Word of God. If a message conflicts with scripture, it does not come from the Lord. The prophet who utters; "thus saith the Lord", but fails to convey God's Word, speaks not for God but for himself. He is fraudulent and misrepresents the Lord. Indeed, false prophets in the OT days, risked their lives when they uttered falsehood."

Let us all say, as Paul: "Yea, woe is unto me, if I preach not the gospel."

Will Jesus Find Faith On Earth?

Someday Jesus will return to earth. He will come in great glory and in certain judgment upon the people of this world.

> "Nevertheless when the Son of man cometh, *shall He find faith* on the earth?" —Luke 18:8

The question is posed in the Scripture above— Will Jesus find faith when He returns? To be sure the problem of rampant faithlessness and unbelief was a problem even when Christ was walking the earth and performing great miracles, even the life-transforming miracle of the complete healing of some who had been decimated by leprosy. In Luke chapter 17 we find Jesus speaking to one of ten lepers He had recently healed and had returned to give him praise and thanks. Jesus asks:

> "Were not the ten cleansed? but where are the nine?" Were there none found that returned to give glory to God, save this stranger. And He said unto him, Arise, go thy way: thy *faith* hath made thee whole." —Lk 17:17-19 (ASV)

Isn't it unbelievable that nine of the ten lepers that had been miraculously healed from head to toe and given a new lease on life (temporally—that is) did not esteem Christ well enough to come and give Him thanks. We could well imagine and even sympathize with these lepers, overwhelmed with happiness, running home to those they loved and showing themselves healed and able once again to hug and kiss their dear wives and children, mothers and fathers— but can we believe the fact that all but one never returned to the one who gave them this great gift of healing?

This is a picture of the state of humanity. By nature men are unthankful and unwilling to give God the praise He deserves. Even in the face of receiving fantastic blessings from His hands, even miraculous healing, they remain unwilling to give God His due adoration. They are too prideful and senseless to thank God for anything. In a word they are faithless. In fact it is only by the grace of God that any man will praise and thank Him. Only by His gift of faith did the one leper return to glorify Jesus. Christ says to him: "Arise, go thy way: thy *faith* hath made thee whole." This is recorded for our benefit.

This word "*faith*" in the greek is *pistis,* and is defined biblically in the Strong's Bible Concordance/Dictionary as: "the persuasion, credence, moral conviction of the truthfulness of God." It is the same *faith* referred to in Luke 18:8 where it is asked "shall He find *faith* on the earth?" The verse tells us that this is what Jesus will be looking for when He returns. This word conveys the concepts of assurance, belief, and fidelity.

"Were there none *found* that returned to give glory to God." (v. 18) This word *found* is *heurisko* in the greek and in the Strong's heurisko (#2147) is defined biblically to mean variously: find, get, obtain, perceive, see. Will the Son of man *heurisko pistis* when He comes? Will He find, perceive, see people manifesting a moral conviction that what God declares is indeed true and trustworty? I am struck by the pessimism I see implicit in this question. I fully believe that the gospel will have its success and all those whom God calls will come in faith to Him but given the burgeoning population of this world it appears that true faith will be rare, only the remnant saved by grace will possess it.

We find the phrase *Son of Man* used by Jesus to describe himself no less than some 80 times in the New Testament. Jesus uses this title for himself more than any other, referring to His Messianic work and personage. In this term He conveys His heavenly exalted origin, His identification with those He came to save and His glorious future coming.

Here are some examples:

Jesus speaks of Himself: "For as Jonas was three days and three nights in the whales belly; so shall the Son of Man be three days and three nights in the heart of the earth. —Mt 12:40

"For the Son of Man is Lord even of the Sabbath day." —Mt 12:8

"The Son of Man shall be betrayed into the hands of men.
                                                        —Mt 17:22

"Even the Son of Man came not to be ministered unto, but to minister, and to give his life a ransom for many." —Mt 20:28

Jesus uses this title to portray His second coming:

"For the Son of Man shall come in the glory of His Father with His angels; and then He shall reward every man according to his works." This will be an unexpected event. —Mt 16:27

"For as lightning cometh out of the east, and shineth even unto the west; so shall also the coming of the Son of Man be." —Mt 24:27

"When the Son of Man shall come in His glory, and all the holy angels with Him, then shall He sit upon the throne of His glory; and before Him shall be gathered all nations: and He shall separate them one from another, as a shepherd divideth his sheep from the goats. He will be coming as judge, restoring righteousness in the world." —Mt 23:31,32

In John's gospel, the Son of man is equal to the Son of God:

"And no man has ascended up to heaven but he that came down from heaven, even the Son of Man which is in heaven....He that believeth on Him is not condemned: but he that believeth not is condemned already, because he hath not believed in the name of the only begotten Son of God." This reveals the divinity, preexistence and heavenly origin of Jesus our King. —Jn 3:13-18

Continuing in the immediate context of Luke's gospel Jesus while speaking to the Pharisees, warns of judgment and the coming days of the Son of Man. He brings to their rememberance Lot's wife and describes those days as that of— people eating, drinking and marrying, until the flood *came*. The same word as in: "Nevertheless when the Son of man *cometh*..." In the greek: *erchomai.*, defined in Strongs #2064 as: to accompany, to appear, to bring, to come or to enter.

Immediately Jesus speaks a parable (v. 18:1) that men should pray and not give up. He describes a beautiful, persistent faith (*pistis*) that is exhibited by a widow who troubles an unjust judge until he yields and pleases her, not for justice sake, but only so that she would stop coming to trouble him. Jesus uses this parable, an earthly story with a heavenly meaning, to illustrate the kind of persistent faith He will seek when He *comes* (erchomai).

Will He find faith when He comes? One man has said:

"The rhetorical question implies that faith will be scarce. Our Lord's words do not predict a general improvement in the spiritual condition of the world before His coming."

Matthew Henry said:

"The question implies a strong negation: No, He will not; He foresees it."

Will He find faith as in the broken and contrite tax collector of the subsequent verses in Luke? Will He find the faith demonstrated by the little children who receive the kingdom in childlike trust? Without faith it is impossible to please God, for he that cometh to God must believe that He is, and that He is the rewarder of them that diligently seek Him.

Jesus has come and will come at various times, in diverse manners, and for different purposes. He came to heal the sick, to give sight to the blind, to save that which was lost, to preach the gospel, to make the lame walk, and to call sinners to repentance...but was He met with faith?

"He came unto His own, and *His own received Him not.*"
—Jn 1:11; Where was the faith?

He came if happily *he might find any fruit* on the fig tree.
—Mk 11:14; Where was the faith?

"I am come in my Fathers name, *and ye receive me not.*"
—Jn 5:43; Where was the faith?

"O Jerusalem, Jerusalem, that killeth the prophets, and stoneth them that are sent unto her! how often would I have gathered thy children together, even as a hen gathereth her chickens under her wings, *and ye would not*!
—Mt 23:37; Where was the faith?

"And Jesus said unto them, A prophet is not without honor, save in his own country, and among his own kin, and in his own house. And *He could there do no mighty work* (because of their unbelief), save that he laid his hands upon a few sick folk, and healed them."
—Mk 6:5; Where was the faith?

So you see that the problem of faithlessness has always been the case. With fallen man there is no faith. Even the inate knowledge of God, inherent in the hearts of all men despite our fallenness (because all men are made in the image of God), is suppressed in the conscience of faithless mankind. The Bible is replete with examples. But God gives liberally to those who ask. He will give the gift of faith to those that seek Him with a broken and contrite heart. Let us remember and be encouraged by the man who came to Jesus for the healing of his son:

> "Teacher, I brought unto thee my son, who hath a dumb spirit; and wheresoever it taketh him, it dasheth him down: and he foameth, and grindeth his teeth, and pineth away: and I spake to thy disciples that they should cast it out; and they were not able. And he answereth them and saith, O faithless generation, how long shall I be with you? how long shall I bear with you? bring him unto me. And they brought him unto him: and when he saw him, straightway the spirit tare him grievously; and he fell on the ground, and wallowed foaming. And he asked his father, How long time is it since this hath come unto him? And he said, From a child. And oft-times it hath cast him both into the fire and into the waters, to destroy him: but if thou canst do anything, have compassion on us, and help us. And Jesus said unto him, If thou canst! All things are possible to him that believeth. Straightway the father of the child cried out, and said, I believe; help thou mine *unbelief* (lack of faith)." —Mark 9:17b-24

But the question remains— "Will He find faith *in you* when He returns?

How Can I Be Made Perfect?

Do you know that we are commanded to be *perfect*?

> Be ye therefore *perfect*, even as your Father which is in heaven is perfect. —Matthew 6:48

Noah was described as perfect—

> "Noah was a just man and *perfect* in his generations, and Noah walked with God." —Genesis 6:9

Abram was commanded to be perfect, and walked before God:

> "And when Abram was ninety years old and nine, the LORD appeared to Abram, and said unto him, I am the Almighty God; walk before me, and be thou *perfect*." —Genesis 17:1

Jesus was (is) perfect and without sin:

> "He is the Rock, his work is *perfect*: for all his ways are judgment: a God of truth and without iniquity, just and right is he." —Dt 32:4

God can make us perfect:

"God is my strength and power: and he maketh my way *perfect*." —2 Samuel 22:33

Perfect people are synonymous with those that keep God's commandments:

Let your heart therefore be *perfect* with the LORD our God, to walk in his statutes, and to keep his commandments.
—1Kings 8:61

So what exactly does it mean to be perfect? You've heard the common expression: "To err is human but to forgive is divine." Isn't it commonly accepted that nobody is perfect; I mean we all make mistakes— right? Is God commanding us to never make a mistake? Does He really expect me to be sinless?

These are natural questions one would ask in considering the larger question of "What is the Bible's definition of being *perfect*?" To accurately understand what God's definiton of being perfect is can only be accomplished by studying how He uses the term in Scripture. Clearly, Christ is declared as being perfect, we've seen that in Deuteronomy 32:4 above because we know that Christ is the Rock and the Rock is perfect. But consider this verse as well:

"Till we all come in the unity of the faith, and of the knowledge of the Son of God, unto a perfect man, unto the measure of the stature of the fulness of Christ." —Ephesians 4:13

So Christ is the measure or standard of what God defines as the perfect man. He is our goal, we are to strive to be as complete as He is, as sinless as He is. But is that possible? Can we achieve that? Well, I hope we know that this kind of standard is impossible for man to achieve left to his own devices. Scripture has told us:

"For all have sinned, and come short of the glory of God;"
—Rom 3:23

And yet we are commanded to be perfect. So how can this be the case? Well, friend there is only one way to be considered perfect by God— and that is to be found "*in Christ*."

When a man is "in Christ" then all that Christ is, all his perfection, is also attributed to that man. When the Father looks at a sinner saved by grace, He sees a perfect man, He sees His perfect Son. So to be perfect you must be in Christ, you must flee to the perfect Rock for shelter and get into Him. To be in Christ is to be in union with Him. In speaking of this union John Murray says, union with Christ is "the central truth of the whole doctrine of salvation."

Being in Christ is synonymous with being saved. Are you saved? Have you sought the mercy of God in Christ for the salvation of your body and soul? If you have then you are abiding in Christ. You are a sinner made perfect. If not, you are presently not in Christ and God sees you as still in your sins guilty before Him and having fallen short of the glory and of the measure of that perfect man, His son the Lord Jesus Christ.

You see then,

> "Therefore if any man be *in Christ*, he is a new creation: old things are passed away; behold, all things are become new."
> —2 Cor 5:17

Those in Christ are described as being a new creation. The old things have passed away and all things have been made new. Our sins are forgiven and remembered no more by God, they are part and parcel with the old that has passed away.

> "What shall we say then? Shall we continue in sin, that grace may abound? God forbid. How shall we, that are dead to sin, live any longer in it? Know you not, that so many of us as were baptized into Jesus Christ were baptized into his death? Therefore we are buried with him by baptism into death: that just as Christ was raised up from the dead by the glory of the Father, even so we also should walk in newness of life. For if we have been united with him in the likeness of his death, we shall be also in the likeness of his resurrection: Knowing this, that our old man is crucified with him, that the body of sin might be destroyed, that we should no longer

serve sin. For he that is dead is freed from sin. Now if we are dead with Christ, we believe that we shall also live with him." —Rom 6:1-8

Wow, there is so much there in Romans 6:1-8 that lengthy books have been written to do it justice, but for our purposes, I want you to see the language of union with Christ, with being *in Christ*. Note that the believer is to sin no more as he has been baptized into Christ, that he has been made a partaker of His death as the believer is spoken of being baptized (made united) into His death. When we accept Chrit's death for us we are mystically united with Him in His death, and also His resurrection to new life! We are raised to new life in Christ! We have perfect union with Him, we are forever united with Him. Halelujah!

Considering this, what should we do?

"Therefore seeing we also are surrounded with so great a cloud of witnesses, let us lay aside every weight, and the sin which does so easily ensnare us, and let us run with patience the race that is set before us. Looking unto Jesus the author *and perfecter* of our faith; who for the joy that was set before him endured the cross, despising the shame, and is seated at the right hand of the throne of God." —Heb 12:1-2

Do you see how we must look unto Jesus the author and perfecter of our faith. Christ is the one who authored the faith within us and He is the one that will perfect our walk of faith. We are made perfect and our faith is made perfect (complete) in Christ. Now read along with me just a bit further into this same 12th chapter of Hebrews where it is written:

"But you have come to Mount Zion, to the heavenly Jerusalem, the city of the living God. You have come to thousands upon thousands of angels in joyful assembly, to the church of the firstborn, whose names are written in heaven. You have come to God, the judge of all men, *to the spirits of righteous men made perfect*, to Jesus the mediator of a new covenant, and to the sprinkled blood that speaks a better word than the blood of Abel." —Heb 12:22-24

As a believer in Jesus Christ you have come to the city of the living God, wherein you have union with Christ, His angels and His church. When we put our faith in Christ we are united with all those whose names are written in heaven— we are included among the righteous men made perfect! Praise God for His great salvation! For His making us perfect in Christ when we could never be perfect because of our sin and unrighteousness; but now we are accepted as righteous!

So understanding how and why we can be made perfect men and women, what should we know about being perfect in Christ? Let us conclude by considering some wonderful truths—

Perfect people fear God:

> "There was a man in the land of Uz, whose name was Job; and that man was perfect and upright, and one that feared God, and eschewed evil." —Job 1:1

Perfect people are forever secure in God:

> "Behold, God will not cast away a perfect man." —Job 8:20

Perfect men will imitate their Savior and grow in likeness with Him:

> "The disciple is not above his master: but every one that is perfect shall be as his master." —Luke 6:40

Perfect men and women will be given a perfect unity one with the other in Christ:

"And the glory which thou gavest me I have given them; that they may be one, even as we are one: I in them, and thou in me, that they may be made perfect in one." —Jn 17:22-24

"Now I beseech you, brethren, by the name of our Lord Jesus Christ, that ye all speak the same thing, and that there be no divisions among you; but that ye be perfectly joined together in the same mind and in the same judgment."
—1 Cor 1:10

Perfect men never return to trusting in themselves for perfection:

"Are ye so foolish? having begun in the Spirit, are ye now made perfect by the flesh?" —Gal 3:3

Perfect men preach, warn and teach the truth so that others may be found perfect in Christ:

"Whom we preach, warning every man, and teaching every man in all wisdom; that we may present every man perfect in Christ Jesus." —Col 1:28

It is Christ's perfect obedience and atoning work on the cross that makes us perfect:

"For by one offering he hath perfected forever them that are sanctified." —Heb 10:14

Though he were a Son, yet learned he obedience by the things which he suffered; And being made perfect, he became the author of eternal salvation unto all them that obey him. —Heb 5:8-10

Perfect men of God need and love His Word knowing that it is the means by which God makes us perfect:

"All scripture is given by inspiration of God, and is profitable for doctrine, for reproof, for correction, for instruction in righteousness. That the man of God may be perfect, thoroughly furnished unto all good works." —2 Tim 3:16-17

Perfect men trust that even trials are God's way of perfecting them:

"Knowing this, that the trying of your faith worketh patience. But let patience have her perfect work, that ye may be perfect and entire, lacking nothing." —Jam 1:3-5

"But the God of all grace, who hath called us unto his eternal glory by Christ Jesus, after that ye have suffered a while, make you perfect, stablish, strengthen, settle you." —1 Pt 5:10

Isn't God perfect? Isn't studying His word a thrill? Do you realize how blessed we are to be able to answer the question "How can I be made perfect?" It is only by God's grace that we were given this understanding; that only by His perfect gift of faith in the perfect righteousness of Christ can we be made perfect. Amen

99% + 1% = WRONG GOSPEL

There are some that say things to the effect of: "Christ has done 99%! Now it's up to you to just do your 1%!" Does that sound good to you? Sadly it's an appealing idea to many. Even those who should know better, don't see the danger in this idea. Too many people who profess to be believers in Jesus Christ accept the idea that Christ did the overwhelming vast majority of what's required to get you to heaven but he leaves the last critical decision to you. They say that God must not violate your free-will. That He requires human responsibility in salvation. That He doesn't want to be the object of anyone's love that doesn't give it freely and uncoerced. They believe that only if a person voluntarily chooses to have Christ as their Savior by a decision of their own heart can such a choice be considered freely made, and that's the only way by which God wants us to love Him. The problem is they cannot prove these ideas from the Bible. There are various names underwhich these ideas parade themselves, but what they all have in common is this— they believe that salvation requires some contribution on the part of the sinner. In that sense they can all be concluded under the umbrella of synergism.

Synergism, with respect to salvation, is any belief that attributes some work of man as complicit with or in cooperation with that work of God so that a man or woman can be saved. It doesn't matter where you draw the line— whether you consider it a 50-50 split between what man does and what God does, or you take the generous position (at least that's what those who believe this suppose it to be) and you give 99% of the credit and glory to God reserving a mere one percent to man's responsibility. It all results in the same thing— it's the wrong gospel!

Wrong? you ask,— isn't that an exageration? A bit alarmist on my part? Well, *any* doctrine of salvation, any so-called "good news" (the word gospel means "good news") that does not give God 100% of the credit and glory for the work of redemption is a false gospel and therefore not really a gospel at all. It will only result in death to those that follow it. Consider Paul the Apostle's vehement warning:

> "But even though we, or an angel from heaven, should preach to you a gospel contrary to that which we have preached to you, *let him be accursed (damned to hell)*. As we have said before, so I say again now, if any man is preaching to you a gospel contrary to that which you received, let him be accursed." —Gal 1:8-9

Those philosophies of men that would claim that mankind has within himself the ability to seek after God, that teach that within fallen man is still a little bit of "good" left and that the will and ability to accept God on His terms is still intact despite being badly damaged by the fall are all terribly mistaken. Hear what God says:

> "As it is written, There is none righteous, no, not one. There is none that understands, there is none that seeks after God. They are all gone out of the way, they are together become unprofitable; there is none that does good, no, not one." —Rom 3:10-12

Did you get that— Nobody seeks after God. Nobody does good, not one single person. *Nobody!* Wouldn't you think that was the final word on the issue. I do, but these deceivers have "clever" ways of arguing their damning philosophies. These people are false prophets who twist the Scripture's clear teaching:

> "And account that the longsuffering of our Lord is salvation; even as our beloved brother Paul also according to the wisdom given unto him has written unto you; As also in all his epistles, speaking in them of these things; in which are some things hard to be understood, which *they that are unlearned and unstable twist, as they do also the other scriptures, unto their own destruction."* —2 Pt 3:15-16

Paul had more to say in a straight-forward, didactic (instructional) manner with respect to the fact that salvation is clearly a work that is all of God's doing (monegistic-the work of one agent) and not of man that wills some contribution to it (synergistic-the work of more than one agent) than any other inspired writer of Holy Scripture. Yet, these "unlearned and unstable" ones twist the Scriptures they do not understand to the result of their own destruction and that of those following after their heresy.

Unless God intervenes and does the saving no man can be saved:

> "Except the Lord of Sabaoth had left us a seed, we had been as Sodoma, and been made like unto Gomorrha". —Rm 9:29

Righteousness (doing that which is right) is an attribute of God only. It is not found in fallen man, as verse 3:10 makes clear— "there is none righteous, no, not one". When God surveyed the world of Noah's day he concluded thusly:

> "And God saw that the wickedness of man was great in the earth, and that every imagination of the thoughts of his heart *was only evil continually.* And the LORD was sorry that he had made man on the earth, and it grieved him to his heart. And the LORD said, I will destroy man whom I have created

from the face of the earth; both man, and beast, and the creeping thing, and the fowls of the air; for I am sorry that I have made them. But Noah found grace in the eyes of the LORD." —Gen 6:5-8

You see, Noah found grace in the eyes of the Lord. Sometimes we forget that Noah was one of those men in whom every imagination of the thoughts of their hearts was only evil continually! He was just as bad as everyone else but God showed a gracious mercy upon him and his family. How God sees us is all that matters. Not how we imagine ourselves to be. Mankind wants to imagine that they're really not all that bad. Even many that accept the notion of sin still cling tenaciously to the notion that there is still something "good" within fallen man.

They believe that unsaved man can and does (albeit infrequently and imperfectly) things that God can be pleased by, but God has declared His thoughts on this matter. *Only evil continually...* remember that! There is no difference between those people destroyed by the God that was grieved by their evil and regretted making them and those people that came from the loins of Noah's family afterwards— all of us! No difference whatsoever! Apart from being the object of God's grace, all any of us do is evil,... continually. How can anyone get around that! There is no ability or desire in fallen man to do what is pleasing to God.

When Adam disobeyed God in the garden he died. Just as God had warned him:

"And the LORD God took the man, and put him into the garden of Eden to work it and to keep it. And the LORD God commanded the man, saying, Of every tree of the garden you may freely eat. But of the tree of the knowledge of good and evil, you shall not eat of it: for in the day that you eat thereof *you shall surely die.*" Gen 2:15-17

He did not drop down dead physically at that very moment, but his separation from God began immediately. His spiritual death had begun as well as his biological clock beginning its countdown to the day when he would indeed breathe his last and return to the dust from which he was made. Adam was the quintessential man. He was created with a nature and will that was uncorrupted by sin. Of any man that ever lived (apart from Christ), Adam had the surest opportunity to consistently will to do that which was right and pleasing to God. Sadly though, he did in fact fall by disobeying God's law and God's clear warning that death would follow.

By Adam's transgression of the law we have all been made subject to the curse upon human nature. We are all born sinners. That is what we *are*, not something we are taught or a virus we catch. It is the fabric of our very nature and therefore no man is immune from death. Henceforth, from Adam onward, every person born into this world, apart from Christ, is conceived with a nature to disobey God's law. The unsaved person cannot exercise a will that operates *un*influenced by a nature bent toward defying God continually.

This is very bad news for everyone of us. But only by accepting the truth of this awful news can we properly value the good news of God's true gospel. The bad news is that there is nothing good in man, no aspect of man's nature has been left unaffected by Adam's fall, certainly not a will to do good, there is no will to do good. We've seen that. There is no righteousness within fallen man. Righteousness is something that God must provide for us.

We need to accept that only by the work of Christ, who obtains a righteous standing before God the Father on behalf of those that will trust entirely in Him can we be saved. Do you believe salvation is entirely a work of God and that you contribute absolutely nothing meritorious to that process? That is the core truth of the gospel. The true gospel. Not the "God did 99% but unless you choose Him you can't be saved" gospel of the devil which is really isn't a gospel of good news but a damnable lie.

Only in Christ can a sinful man be perfect. God needs to decree or declare us righteous even though sin is ever present in us. This is justification, which is God declaring you righteous for Christ's sake, and based entirely on a sacrifice Christ made on your behalf two thousand years ago and based upon a decision that was made within the Godhead before the foundation of the world. What part of that can you take credit for?

There was a Savior before there was a sinner. There was a salvation plan before there was a fall. We cannot separate God from His saving work. God is the gospel. "The Lord *is* my light and salvation." He *is* our righteousness, and He *is* our salvation. He *is* the truth, and He *is* the light of the world. We are only saved through a connection with Christ that He reaches down from heaven to give us. He is the originator and initiator of love, grace and mercy.

This completely independent nature of God is known as His sovereignty. God is in no way *ever* obligated to man or contingent in his decisions or actions upon the will of man. Those that say He must respect the will of man are deceivers. They have made an idol of the will of man and worship it above the sovereign creator of that man and his will. They deny the consequence of the death that God promised and executed upon man for Adam's transgression. They artificially create a doctrine that fallen man still retains enough of a function of his will that he still has the ability and the inclination to seek after and choose God. But this is a false doctrine that cannot be proven from Scripture. If it were true then the man that chooses God has something about him that he can point to that distinguishes him from the man that didn't choose to follow God, namely that he exercised his will to do so while others didn't. This is that 1% that they reserve to themselves in their false doctrine of salvation. That is their boast. Listen to what God says—

"For who maketh thee to differ from another? And what hast thou that thou didst not receive? Now if thou didst receive it, why dost thou glory, as if thou hadst not received it?"
—1 Cor 4:7

You see those that think they differ from others in that they made themselves to differ by the exercise of their own will have something they can boast of. They have stolen that 1% of glory from God and kept it for themselves. It is their supposed free-will that gives them the glory. Listen to what Martin Luther, the Reformer said on this matter:

"If any man doth ascribe aught of salvation, even the very least, to the free-will of man, he knoweth nothing of grace, and he hath not learnt Jesus Christ aright."

Do not bring God down to your level, as if we could do something of ourselves to work with God in our salvation. Instead, give Him all the glory. Know the God of Scripture. Know what man is rightly, and how utterly incapable of choosing God we are unless He first chooses to do a work in us. We cannot call upon Him whom we have not known. Know the Savior. Know His work which justified you. Know His resurrection. Don't ever think that it was not completely finished as He declared upon the cross. If it was completely paid in full then what need does God have for you to contribute to it? Rest in the completely accomplished work of Christ, receive it for the unmerited gift that it is and bow to your sovereign Lord and thank Him. It was done for those who know their unworthiness by a sovereign God who took the initiative and...

"while we were yet sinners, (Christ) died for us." —Rom 5:8

Many will compromise the plain truth by proclaiming that division in the church is caused by an unbending insistence upon the total sovereignty of God. They ridicule the notion that they may not have had all truth revealed to them in the face of our attempts at correcting their notions that they contributed to their salvation no matter how small they make that contribution.

Augustine rightly said:

> "Apart from the regenerating work of the Holy Spirit that God performs in the souls of the elect, no person in his own power, is able to choose Godliness, to choose Christ or choose the things of God."

May we all say as the Reformers of old did: *Soli Deo Gloria*, which is— *To God Alone Be All The Glory!*

Restoring the Fallen
When Sin Rears Its Ugly Head

Sadly, in the corporate life of many churches, there are episodes when gross sin rears it's ugly face, and some fall so badly that we question if they were ever saved to begin with. It can really shake people up especially when the one who falls into sin is a pastor or elder. We read or hear accounts in the headlines far too often of what are deemed "moral" failures and such public sin brings disgrace upon Christ, His message and His church. Through these failures those unbelievers outside the church are emboldened to doubt and ridicule the things of God:

> "You that say a man should not commit adultery, do you commit adultery? you that abhor idols, do you commit sacrilege? You that make your boast of the law, through breaking the law do you dishonor God? For *the name of God is blasphemed among the Gentiles through you*, as it is written." —Rom 2:22-24

But what should our reaction be to the one who has brought such disgrace? Having lived through just such an episode in the life of my church while serving as an elder I hope I can bring some useful counsel. Firstly, the natural questions that strike so many in the congregation are— "Can this person really be a Christian?" "How can a blood-bought, Spirit-filled believer do such a thing?" I think it's only natural to ask such questions. It's our way of expressing the horror that such sin really is and how horrible it is when it is finally exposed by God and made public. The pain and disappointment is so fresh that we often make the snap decision that this person was none of God's, and then we recall how blessed we were by them for so long, and we become seriously conflicted in our hearts. I think that it is best to try to reserve such judgments at the start, as the true answers to such questions may or may not be revealed to our understanding. We must remember that God alone knows the heart but we are responsible to act in accordance with His word despite the hurt and turmoil.

Our first obligation is to consider ourselves and to realize that but for the grace of God we too are capable of falling in so horrendous a manner. This is not to minimize in anyway the sin this person has committed or its damaging effects but rather to check what are often self-righteous thoughts along the lines of "How could they have done that?" and "I would never commit so horrible a sin!",— but listen to God's warning to us when we witness such circumstances:

> "Brethren, if a man be overtaken in a fault, you who are spiritual, restore such a one in the spirit of meekness; *considering yourself, lest you also be tempted.* Bear you one another's burdens, and so fulfill the law of Christ. For if a man thinks himself to be something, when he is nothing, he deceives himself." —Gal 6:1-3

God puts us in our place when we have those thoughts of spiritual superiority when He says "For if a man thinks himself to be something, when he is nothing, he deceives himself." We are warned against thinking we somehow differ from the person in question and are above sinning in so heinous a way— if we do, God says we deceive ourselves and are ignorant to our true vulnerability. When we see someone fall in so gross and public a manner we should thank God that He has thus far preserved us from such public shame. How many of us, if we are honest, can recall sins we have comitted that were they to be made known would bring us great embarassment. Sober introspection should humble us and cause us to cling all the more to our Savior in meek reliance upon Him. For only by His grace are we not in a similar place.

Considering our own frailty should prepare our hearts to be ready and willing to act, to whatever degree it is in our power, to help the sinner to be restored to God and the church. Now it is true that the degree to which restoration can and will occur does rely chiefly on the ones involved in the sin. If there is true repentance exhibited, we must be ready to forgive. We will share the burden and contribute to restoration in meekness. When there is sincere repentance shown by the sinner we know God is at work in that person's heart and He desires the sinner's restoration.

Restoration has many considerations. When, for instance, we talk of restoring a building after an earthquake, we don't mean to merely restore it to its pre-quake condition, as that would be short-sighted. It is not enough just to repair the building. It must be made stronger than it was before the quake. Improvements must be made so it doesn't crumble with the next occurrence. In the same way we must seek to restore the repentant one in a way that will make them stronger in Christ than they were before. This can take many forms and will look differently in each situation, so we need much wisdom. The one we seek to restore must be held accountable in love, and that may often include the necessary and immediate loss of position or even autonomy within the church. A person may no longer be permitted to be in the company of the opposite gender, without others present, when the sin was sexual in nature. This is not to degrade them but to provide measures of safety and accountability.

Often the spiritual needs of this person in the process of restoration can exceed the scope of care usually provided by a church. It may require the need for outside help from a Christian counselor who is experienced in biblical counseling and the process of restoration while having none of the bias that may come as a consequence of being part of the local church in which the sin occurred. At the very least, in cases where the restoration process can be faithfully handled within the local church body, it will require a group of mature Christians acting as an Intensive Care Unit. The goal being a restorative process of returning the one to fellowship with God, family and fellow believers. It is no easy prospect. Such a process has its challenges to all involved: faith can be challenged, the collateral damages resulting from the sin must be dealt with, and a recovery/restoration process may also be necessary to help those hurt by the sin.

What we absolutely must avoid is a knee-jerk reaction to shoot our wounded or abandon those whose behavior brought the scandal upon the church. We can too easily react in our flesh and manifest anger towards the person who disappointed us and brought shame upon our church. We can deride and gossip, and justify it for its assumed cathartic relief. I can tell you from experience that such anger cannot work the righteousness of God. I'm not talking of the anger we are to righteously feel when appropriate but rather how we deal with those feelings as we interact with others in the body and as we react as a corporate entity.

We should rather bring hope and provide guidance while still demanding honesty and repentance. Galatians 6:1 requires those who are spiritual, to restore gently. Often a church is ill-equipped to deal with grievous sin made public, especially if they have never had to deal with it previously in their history. Churches can make any number of serious mistakes that complicate the matter and add sin upon sin. Three common incorrect approaches are:

1. Immediately casting the sinner out.
2. Ignoring or denying the sin.
3. Exercising a "Forgive and forget" approach that does not require the accountability of true repentance.

All the above are commonly resorted to as "quick fixes" that do nothing to remedy the problems. They leave out true restoration which has as its primary goal bringing the offender back to a right relationship with God and his Christian brethren. Restoration usually requires discipline and guidance (which includes grace on the part of the church), and necessarily holding those that sinned responsible to God and to those hurt by their sin. Casting the sinner out cannot accomplish these goals.

We need to deal with the full truth regarding the sin, we cannot ignore, excuse or deny the sin that occurred. Sticking our heads in the sand does nothing to effect complete repentance, establish spiritual principles and disciplines, or to restore damaged relationships. These challenges are equally avoided by an unbiblical approach of "forgiving and forgetting." To quickly declare our "forgiveness" before a sober and ordered process of restoration and a confirmation of biblical repentance has genuinely occurred is not a proper God-honoring response. Christians can mistakenly believe that being quick to forgive is what God expects but when this is done without holding the one that sinned accountable it is not. They may think that they are obligated to "forget" the sin, and that a process requiring accountability is unnecessarily harsh and unkind. This cannot be further from the truth.

God's word is true, and He will not let unrepented of sin go without consequences to the one who offended and the church that does not hold him accountable. He is faithful, though, to remain in our presence and give grace when we acknowledge and confess our sin and seek to do all that is within our power to make amends for the damage our sin has caused. Restoration requires deliberate involvement. Listen kindly and acknowledge the seriousness of the sin, rather than assist in the destruction that denial brings. Does God help those who do not want to face themselves or their sin? Does He aid in a cover-up or in efforts to protect the offender from consequences?

For answers to such questions I can point you to a highly recommended book: *Restoring the Fallen: A Team Approach to Caring, Confronting and Reconciling* by Earl & Sandy Wilson, Paul & Virginia Friesen, and Larry & Nancy Paulson. Please get it, read it, and pray through it as we have a lot of learning to do. Let's look inward and upward as we read its counsel:

> "You might ask, "Why? Why can't we just forgive and forget? Why can't we just move on?" The answer is that I, as a sinner, have spent hours, days, possibly years denying the truth that my sin has consequences for me, for those I have sinned against and for innocent bystanders. I do not need to be continually confronted with what I've done, but neither should I be allowed to deny the impact my sin has had on me and others or to slip back into familiar sinful ways. God lets me, and all of us, remember our sins and the consequences so that we will not return to them. Complete restoration is impeded when we don't help wayward Christians examine the full extent of the shambles their sin has caused." — from *Restoring the Fallen*

A sinner can choose to either: 1) not repent, or feign repentance, and receive a pseudo-restoration, or, 2) repent biblically, and pursue a course to be truly restored.

Keeping in mind that we are all sinners necessitates that we not simply think of the above quote with respect to others. Let's look at something from L.R. Shelton Jr., who borrowed many of his ideas from Arthur W. Pink—

"Where are the sinners crying unto God for mercy? Where is the convicting power of the Holy Spirit? Where are the prayer meetings, the praise meetings, the separation from the world? Where is the exalting and lifting up of Christ among His people?

Where is our new life of holiness and the vital godliness that makes us bond slaves to Jesus Christ? The problem is that many have rushed into profession without the slightest bit of work in their hearts by the Holy Spirit."

To my brothers and sisters in Christ I say— We need to understand God's hatred for our sin, and examine our hearts honestly before God; acknowledging the need for His mercy. If we believe that all things work for good for those that are called of God then we can understand that what seems to be a disaster in our church can eventually be an unforeseen blessing from our loving God. Sin exposed and repented of is the will of God for us all. In our church it is already making broken families well again for those who have repented of their part in the sinful scandal. It is causing us as a church body to look inwardly for strength, and to God's word for truth and approval, rather than to our fallen elder. We are working together as never before with a greater purpose, while seeking our God for his power and grace.

I know God's will and plans are always correct, and they work for the good of His saints. We will look back, as I have many times in my Christian life, and say: "Lord thank you, for giving me the opportunity to see and experience all this. Thank you for giving me the faith, desire and grace to be a part of your great plan." He will build His church, and the gates of hell will not prevail.

Where Is Christ in The Midst of Our Disappointment?

God, who is not a liar as we are, has promised never to leave nor forsake us. I cling to that promise in the midst of my disappointments, and I believe it along with the fact that all things are working together for my good, even when I don't see it.

Maurice Roberts makes the point:

> "The Christian life would be a path of roses if God never called us to suffer any disappointments".

He points out setbacks as being common to most biblical characters, and that it is immaturity revealed in the believer who would expect to be free from disappointments. Even our Savior displayed His disappointment when He lamented: "O Jerusalem, Jerusalem... how often I have longed to gather thy children together...!" and Isaiah groaned: "Lord, how long?" Roberts reminds us that although the Messiah experienced disappointment among His own Jewish people, He went on to have great success among the Gentiles. Disappointment is common to all, and is even experienced by those most holy and obedient to God.

I am encouraged as I see our church teams working and improving things, restoring Wednesday night praise, and I look forward to everything coming together for Christ's glory; we are purer, and wiser after our great disappointment. So what can we look forward to? I'm sure many of you are asking— What Now?

The author Philip Crosby is known for saying: "If anything is certain, it is that change is certain." He goes on to observe: "The world we are planning for today will not exist in this form tomorrow". Change is unsettling. Tomorrow is uncertain.

As our lives and relationships change, sometimes we laugh, and sometimes we cry. Carl Sandberg said: "Life is like an onion, you peel a layer at a time, and sometimes you cry." As we live out the Christian life, we see God ordained directions we must take. He sometimes leads us away from the familiar and loved, and tests our comfort level and obedience. We know however, that when we are given a light, we must let it shine forth; when given a talent, we must use it to God's glory and for His will. He challenges us to follow when called, testing our obedience; our desire for comfort and pleasure must be put aside— even if sometimes we cry.

Hebrews tells us:

> "...be without covetousness, and be content with such things as ye have: for He hath said, I will never leave thee."

Saints, times may be challenging but we have everything we need! We have been blessed with provision but more importantly we have been blessed with Christ's own dear presence to cheer and to guide! Change may be a certainty, but through it all, we have the Rock that stands in the midst of us, declaring: "Peace be unto you." We have a Savior that is "Jesus Christ, the same yesterday, and today, and forever!" What a joy by which we may be strengthened and "...comfort (y)ourselves together, and edify one another", because we know that where the church is, He is also! Christ our Lord and friend is right beside us in our disappointment; He is sovereign over all the change.

God ordained the trials of Job but Job eventually experienced restoration in his life. We must sometimes rest patiently in the Lord trusting that what may appear at the moment to be a "no" from God may only be a "wait." There are no final disappointments for the believer. Don't be too hasty to conclude that you know how God is dealing with you. Be still and know that He is God. His will unfolds as He unfolds it— let patience have its perfect work. Hope in the Lord, it is difficult but He will not disappoint.

"Hope deferred maketh the heart sick, but when the desire cometh it is a tree of life". —Prv 13:12

Our church is just now turning a corner and overcoming a dark day, but with Christ in our midst we will see a bright and better tomorrow! Remember

"Unto the upright there ariseth light in the darkness; He is gracious and full of compassion..." —Ps 112:4b

Rely more heavily upon the means of grace, namely— prayer, bible study, hearing the Word preached, fellowshipping with the saints, the Lord's Supper, the singing of psalms and hymns and spiritual songs. These are all gifts from God given to us for our comfort and edification. They each minister to us through our days of disappointment, uncertainty and change. The Word read or preached is Christ in our midst, communing in fellowship with the saints is Christ in our midst, when we pray together Christ is in our midst.

As we improve in holiness, correct our course, and please our Lord as never before by working forward in love and humility we do so only by the power of Christ in our midst. Don't doubt for a second that we will not only survive our trial, but thrive and grow into a sweeter, more holy, and more honest temple for our God. No longer merely babes surviving, but mature ones thriving; loving and sharing our God in the bonds of unity. The dust will settle and we will find that all along He was right there in our midst.

Judge or Savior—Who and When

To a man that requested that Jesus tell his brother to divide the family inheritance with him Jesus replied:

> "Man, *who appointed Me a Judge or an arbiter* between you?"—Lk 12:14

Elsewhere we read:

> "For the Father judgeth no man, but *hath committed all judgment unto the Son.*" —Jn 5:22

Jesus goes on to say:

> "I can of Mine own self do nothing; as I hear, *I judge and my judgment is just;* because I seek not Mine own will, but the will of the Father which hath sent me." —Jn 5:30

> "...and yet *if I judge, My judgment is true.*" —Jn 8:16

And then there is the curious account of the woman dragged to Christ and accused of adultery to which, after her accusers had all left, Christ says:

> "...'Woman, where are those thine accusers? did no one pass sentence upon thee?' and she said, 'No one, Sir;' and Jesus said to her, '*Neither do I pass sentence on thee*; be going on,

and no more sin.'" —Jn 8:10b-11 (Young's Literal Translation)

Are you confused yet? Is Jesus a judge or is He not? To further confuse, Peter writes:

"And if ye call on the Father, who without respect of persons judgeth according to every man's work, pass the time of your sojourning here in fear." —1Pt 1:17

But I thought John 5:22 taught that the Father had committed all judgment into the Son's hands? If that's not enough to perplex you later in the gospel of John we read of Jesus speaking:

"And if anyone hears my sayings but does not keep them, it is not I that judge him, for *I did not come in order to judge the world* but in order to save the world. He who rejects Me and does not receive My sayings has one that judges him. *The Word* which I have spoken, that *will judge him on the last day*."
—Jn 12: 47-48

Does the Father judge? Does Jesus judge? or Does the Word judge? A study that might begin to do justice to these questions could easily fill an entire book but we can't possibly touch on all that there is to this matter in only a few pages. What I can do is give you the brass tacks. So let's begin with the Word.

The first thing we learn from the book of John, is that:

"In the beginning was the Word, and the Word was with God, and the Word was God." —Jn 1:1

"And the Word was made flesh, and dwelt among us, (and we beheld his glory, the glory as of the only begotten of the Father,) full of grace and truth." —Jn 1:14

So we see that Jesus is the Word and that the Word was with God and the Word was God. Remember from John 12:48b quoted above that it is the Word that judges on the last day. So we see that

Jesus, who is the Word, is spoken of as exercising judgment on the last day—

> "I charge thee therefore before God, and the Lord Jesus Christ, *who shall judge the quick and the dead at His appearing and His kingdom.*" —2 Tm 4:1

His appearing to judge is synonymous with the last day and is a reference to when Christ returns in the future. He will return for the purpose of rendering the final judgment of God upon the whole human race and it will be his Word previously spoken to us through the law and the prophets and the Apostles that will be used to judge us. We will either be found in Christ and safe from the condemnation that our breaking of His word requires, or we will be found with no protection, and the Word will exact its stated penalty for lawbreaking,— which is death. Eternal death in hell.

Praise God that it is still the day of salvation! For until that final day when Jesus returns to judge the world in righteous judgment, He has come not to exact judgment but to seek those who are lost and be a Savior to those who heed His Word. While it is light and we have life, we still have the Savior who uses His Word to bring us to himself.

John tells us in 1 John, that the Father sent the Son to be the Savior of the world. He says that there are three that bear record in heaven: the Father, the Word, and the Holy Ghost, and that these three are One. The trinity is working in chorus to save a people unto God. By the inspiration of the Holy Spirit we read:

> "Whosoever transgresseth, and abide not in the doctrine of Christ, hath not God. He that abideth in the doctrine of Christ, he hath both Father and Son." —2 Jn 1:9

Clearly, when Jesus came in His incarnation the first time, His mission and role was that of Savior. His life and Word were left to us as an example of how we are to live. His gospel reveals how we may be saved because we have all sinned and fallen short of the glory of God. We need to submit now before we meet Christ when He returns as Judge of the living and the dead.

"Kiss the Son, lest He be angry and you be destroyed in your way, for His wrath can flare up in a moment. blessed are all who take refuge in Him." —Ps 2:12

"For it is written, As I live, says the Lord, every knee shall bow to me, and every tongue shall confess to God. So then every one of us shall give account of himself to God.
—Rom 14:11-12

We know every knee will bow, but let's pray that we, and all who we love, bow to Him this side of judgment day.

"Yet a little while is the light with you. Walk while you have the light, lest darkness overtake you. He who is walking in the darkness does not know where he is going. While you have the light, believe in the light, in order that you may become the sons of light." —Jn 12:35-36

"I am come a light into the world, that whosoever believes on me should not abide in darkness." —Jn 12:46

"You are all sons of the light and sons of the day. We do not belong to the night or to the darkness." —1 Thes 5:5

"...blessed are they that hear the Word of God and keep it."
—Lk 11:28

And so today, while we are alive and can still hear the Word, it is the day of salvation. Today we may have a Savior before He will return as the Righteous Judge of the world. If we are in Christ now we will have nothing to fear when He returns in judgment.

You've read about the door of the ark being shut once and for all and how all that were without perished. Those that entered the ark did so by faith. Get into the ark who is Christ before the door is finally shut— for then it will be too late.

What's in a Name?

Our church's name is Grace Gospel Church.

So I ask— Do we indeed have a biblical notion of what grace is? I remember watching a Bill Moyer's special called *Amazing Grace*. It showcased many renditions of the famous hymn by thrilling singers. That part was enjoyable. What was painful to watch was when countless people were asked what does "grace" mean to them. Moyer must have asked at least 25 people the question, and yet I can only remember one person giving an answer that began to get at the biblical definition of grace. Since John Newton wrote his famous hymn to extol the magnificent grace of God in saving him— a lost sinner; we need to answer that question from the Word of God. Unfortunately, despite "loving" the hymn, everyone else that was asked to define "grace" as they understood it gave an answer that was worldly and completely ignorant of the history of the hymn, of John Newton's story, and worst of all, of the Bible.

By the world's definitions, grace is a disposition to act with kindness or clemency, perhaps to grant a reprieve; grace is often considered composure under pressure. Grace can be a charming quality or trait or a pleasing appearance. It is a short prayer prior to a meal, asking a blessing or giving thanks. All of these are legitimate definitions but they are not what Christians have in mind or should have in mind when we use the term "Grace". We all know the name Grace Gospel Church was not chosen to communicate any of those more general definitions of grace. It was our choice to declare by the use of the word *grace*, all that God has to say about it.

As we study the Word of God we learn that the best defnition of *grace* is the *unmerited favor of God towards undeserving sinners*. Grace is the act of God bestowing a saving love upon men and women who have done nothing to merit it, and have, in fact, done everything to deserve the righteous punishment and judgment of God. The grace of God is goodness on God's part that requires that He does everything on behalf of unrighteous, undeserving men. He must solve the problem of enmity, which is mutual hatred. You see, we hate God, and He hates sinners, and yet He still gives grace to those He has chosen to save. The whole process of salvation is a gracious act of God. From His decision to save certain men and women by taking them out of their sinful course towards eternal damnation (predestination/election); to the payment of their sins (redemption); to the gift of the Spirit which seals and grows them in holiness (sanctification); to the temporal gifts and blessings that make life enjoyable. Someday He will also save us from the presence of sin by removing it from our lives for all of eternity and making us fit to inhabit heaven (glorification). All these amazing acts of goodness are each completely undeserved, but He does them all for those He saves! Grace upon grace!

> "For the grace of God that bringeth salvation hath appeared to all men." —Titus 2:11

We can never plumb the depths of God's grace to us, but God gives us this description,—

> "For we know the grace of our Lord Jesus Christ, that, though he was rich, yet for your sake he became poor, that ye through His poverty might be rich." —2 Cor 8:9

How rich He was in glory, He had everything! He had his sterling reputation. He had never experienced the shame for wrongdoing, and yet He volunteered to give everything up for our sake. He was willing to become poor for us and to suffer the insults of sinners against Him and the shame and noteriety of being branded a sinner. How poor he became because of our sin. How rich we became as the "sons of God" and "heirs of God" through His humiliation. This is the salvation that grace brings.

At Grace Gospel Church we must never forget this grace. We need to constantly be reminded of this incredible grace for which we named our church. Being human we are prone to forget, it is almost too frightening to remember because we must again come to grips with our depravity and unworthiness to properly consider such undeserved goodness. But the Spirit presses us to ponder anew all that the Almighty can do (and has done) for us. We must work at remembering. This is not burdensome but glorious to revel in the love and charity of so gracious a God. At Grace Gospel Church we must look ahead in anticipation of our blessed hope—

"Looking for that blessed hope, and the glorious appearing of the great God and our Saviour Jesus Christ; Who gave himself for us, that he might redeem us from all iniquity, and purify unto himself a peculiar people, zealous of good works."
—Titus 2:13-14

We ask:

"Why have I found grace in your eyes, that thou should take knowledge of me, seeing I am a stranger?" —Ruth 2:10

Why have we found grace in Your eyes? "Amazing love! How can it be,—that thou my God should die for me!" He knew us! He loved us! He saved us! We were dead and He made us alive! We couldn't even see the kingdom until He gave us new birth! Without His grace we could do nothing but be judged and cast into hell!

"Who hath saved us, and called us with a holy calling, not according to *our works*, but according to His own purpose and *grace* which was *given* us in Christ before the world began." —2 Tim 1:9

"But God, who is rich in mercy, for His great love wherewith He loved us, even when we were dead in sins, hath quickened us (made us spiritually alive) together with Christ, and hath raised us together, and made us to sit together in heavenly places in Christ Jesus; that in the ages to come He might show the exceeding *riches of His grace* in *His kindness* toward us through Christ Jesus. For *by grace are ye saved* through faith; and not of yourselves: it is *the gift* of God." —Eph 2:4-8

So what's in a name... everything for which we give thanks!

Go?

God speaks in the fifth chapter of Matthew:

> "Therefore if thou bring thy gift to the altar, and there rememberest that thy brother hath ought against thee; Leave there thy gift before the altar, and go thy way; first be reconciled to thy brother, and then come and offer thy gift."
> —Mt 5:23-24

So, when we are *the offender* we are *to go to our brother* whom we've offended *and seek to be reconciled*. Got it!

In Matthew 18 we read:

> "Moreover if thy brother shall trespass against thee, go and tell him his fault between thee and him alone: if he shall hear thee, thou hast gained thy brother." Mt 18:15

So, when we are *the offended,* we are *to go to our brother* who has offended us *and seek to be reconciled*. But I thought God said in Matthew 5 that it's the one who is the *offender* that's supposed to go to the other! So is he coming or am I going? It looks like I'm going in both cases. Isn't that interesting— regardless of whether I am the offender or the one offended God requires that I go to my brother and seek to be reconciled. So in any conflict both parties are expected to be the one to go. Neither one can comfortably sit and have the attitude: "Well, he is the one that sinned against me let him be the one to come asking for forgiveness!" It seems either way, I am to reconcile and gain my brother. I guess we're not vindicated before God by just thinking we're the one in the right, but we need to move.

How about the prodigal coming to his senses and seeing he had sinned against Heaven and his father? He arose and went to his father, but didn't the father, as soon as he saw his son, drop everything and come and running to him while he was yet running to the father? What a beautiful picture? It really goes to answering the question of who was to go to whom?

Now, when Jacob starts out to go to Esau, he was afraid and distressed, but who was it that came to Jacob, running like the prodigal's father, embracing Jacob and falling on his neck, while kissing him and weeping?

How many of us are separated from someone that God demands we be reconciled to? Is it enough to feel you're right? Even to know that you did nothing that warranted the offense? Doesn't the world need to see we are disciples by witnessing our love towards one another? It seems God is as interested in reconciliation as he is upon establishing the blame. Sure, if we are the offender we must confess our offense to our brother and seek his forgiveness, but we need to do that whether we get to him first or he gets to us first—either way we have met.

In his book, *The Mark of a Christian*, Francis A. Schaeffer explains there is a way we can exhibit love without sharing in our brother's mistake: by approaching the problem with a desire to solve it, rather than a desire to win. A solution gives God the glory.

> "So whether you eat or drink or *whatever you do, do it all for the glory of God.*" 1 Cor 10:31

So, even though we may be reluctant to go and seek our brother, we know that, right or wrong, if we go, we are on the path to pleasing

God. It seems, by the examples given above, that God wants both parties take the initiative in going. If we were truly obedient to Christ we would be bumping into each other as we are each seeking to be reconciled to the other regardless of who did the sinning. In reality its often the case that the fault does not necessarily lie completely with one versus the other party but that once there was an offence both parties added to the initial offence and so both have a reason to go and confess their sin and seek reconciliation. God leaves us truly without any excuse for inaction doesn't he?

Go to your brother now! Show mercy and grace, and you will please the God who loves the peacemakers. Fear not, and remember that Christians are like teabags: Their real strength comes out when they get into hot water. E.M. Poteat wrote: "The forces of good in the world are immobilized less by their adversaries, than by their sleep (inaction)."

Often division between brethren is corporate in nature and can come as the result of differences in our interpretation of Scripture or of practice within the church. A cursory perusal of church history will yield countless examples of church splits and schisms resulting in entirely new denominations. I'm sure not a few of these were valid and necessary actions that men of conviction reluctantly took in the face of unorthodoxy or liberalism, but how many were simply mountains made into molehills by the pride of men too self-justified to work at harmony and reconciliation.

Maurice Roberts warns: "Perfect harmony among God's people is not to be expected before we get to heaven." He correctly points out that there exists differing degrees of sanctification between us, that we have trouble esteeming others better than ourselves, and that we frequently fail to forebear with one another in non-essential differences as we should. Too many become wise in their own eyes, and Roberts says: "It is a thousand pities when (non-essential) differences become the occasion of alienating brethren from one another."

John Owens said it best:

> "I confess I would rather, spend all my time and days in making up and healing the breaches that are amongst Christians than one hour in justifying our divisions....Who is sufficient for such an attempt? The closing of differences amongst Christians is like opening the book of Revelation...there is none able or worthy to do it, in heaven or in earth, except The Lamb: when He will put forth the greatness of His power for it, it shall be accomplished, and not before. In the meantime, a reconciliation amongst all Protestants is our duty. When men have labored as much in the improvement of the principle of forbearance as they have done to subdue other men to their opinions, religion will have another appearance in the world."

So there we have it. To whatever degree it is within our power to be at peace with all men we must, as the Scripture says:

> "If possible, so far as it depends on you, live in peace with all people." Rom 12:18 (ISV)

I like Owens thoughts on this. When men have worked just as hard at the practice of patiently forebearing with those that differ with them than they have at doggedly trying to persuade others to their way of thinking, the church of God will have a wholly other appearance than it presently does. But the latter half of his quote speaks to the daunting task of doing so. With man it is impossible, but with the help of the Lamb all things are possible. Why do we let it go so far? It's pride and a lack of humility isn't it? Whether we're dealing with doctrinal divisions within the church or differences borne out of our sin against a brother, God would have us strive toward peace and unity. We are to go quickly and seek reconciliation before it becomes too hard.

> "A brother offended is harder to be won than a strong city: and such contentions are like the bars of a castle." —Pr 18:19

So...Go! Don't be afraid,— it's your *direction*, not your *perfection*.

Am I Saved By How I Feel or By What Christ Has Done?

"Therefore being justified by faith, we *have peace* with God *through* our Lord Jesus Christ." —Rm 5:1

Consider another translation of this verse:

"Therefore, since we have been made right in God's sight by faith, we have peace with God because of what Jesus Christ our Lord has done for us." —Rm 5:1 (NLT)

I like the way we can really see the past-tense nature of what Christ has already accomplished for us in the above translation: "we *have been made* right" "because of what Jesus...*has done* for us."

This is the heart of the gospel of grace. Our salvation was accomplished in full for us before we were ever born. The choice to save us was made by God before even the world was made! Wow! If we have been saved we are no longer at war with God. This is not a subjective truth based on any requirement that we feel or sense it. We do not "make it true" for us by agreeing to it or because the idea appeals to us. It is true because God has said it is true! I am so glad it doesn't come down to a feeling which can't always be trusted, but a promise from a God who cannot lie.

We stand in the presence of a Holy God who has given to His people access to Him and we rejoice, not doubting, in the hope of the glory of God. Our hope is not a vague feeling of "Oh, I really hope this will happen" but a confident assured "knowing" that what God promises He will deliver. Rejoice in the fact that wherever you are today, one of the benefits of having been justified is the hope that one day we shall be like Him. He has guaranteed it.

> "Beloved (yes, He loves you today) now are we the sons of God (members of His family by our new birth) and it doth not yet appear what we shall be: but we know that, (are confidently assured) when He shall appear, we shall be like Him, for we shall see Him as He is. And every man that hath this hope in Him purifieth himself, (we definitely *do* purify ourselves, not we might purify ourselves) even as He is pure." —1 Jn 3:2,3

We have received God's promise of complete glorification— we shall be like Him. Our complete deliverance and sanctification is the purpose of God.

So brethren there will be times when you may not feel saved, and Satan will gladly confirm those feelings, but God implores you: "You've trusted in Jesus alone, He did it all, you have been saved, I am faithful, do not fear for I am with thee, be not dismayed, I am thy God, when you pass through the waters, I will be with you, I will uphold you, I am the Hope of Glory, turn your eyes on me your blessed assurance." Brothers and sisters— we have been called to holiness, not to doubt.

> "These things have I written to *you* that believe on the name of the Son of God; that *you* may *know* that you have eternal life, and that you may *believe* on the name of the Son of God. —1 Jn 5:13

"...that you may *know* that you have eternal life,..." This knowledge is *assurance* regarding our salvation and eternal life. Let me say it with a different emphasis: this heartfelt knowledge *is* assurance! Do you believe these truths?— then let that be your assurance— not how you feel about your performance. I find it very interesting that in place of a benediction he exhorts:

"Little children, keep yourselves from idols". —1 Jn 5:21

Do we allow doubt to overwhelm us? While every Christian will have doubts on occasion, we must understand that doubt is a form of unbelief. Doubt is a retreat back to looking at ourselves as the author and finisher of our salvation. It either depends upon us or God, right? We ponder our sinfulness and how far we are from living the image of Christ to a watching world and revert to thoughts of whether we are good enough to be accepted by God. This is idolatry. We may even go so far as to renew our efforts to cleanse ourselves by trying harder to be holy and obedient to God— our *already cleansed selves!* When doubt strikes we must go back into the Word and read how it does not depend on our performance but by the completely accomplished work of Christ on the behalf of those who believe His promises. Did you believe Christ? Do you believe Christ? Are you still trusting that Christ is perfect and will not fail? Then, little children, keep yourselves from the idol of your own performance and trust in the performance of Christ. In a never ending state of doubt, we are useless to do God's work. How can we—

"Go into all the world, and preach the *Good News* to everyone." —Mk 16:15-16 (NLT)

when we consider ourselves unacceptable and inadequate? Are we still nursing our idol of self— "...but I am not worthy!" I ask you— When were you ever worthy?

"And we know (have assurance) that the Son of God is come, and hath given us an understanding, that we may know Him that is true, (all His work and promises are true and trustworthy) and we are in Him that is true, (if we are in Him then it does not depend upon us) even in His Son Jesus Christ. This is the true God, (not an idol of our own making) and eternal life. —1 Jn 5:20

So brethren...

"Let us draw near with a true heart in *full assurance* of faith, having our hearts sprinkled from an evil conscience (only God cleanses the heart), and our bodies washed with pure water. Let us *hold fast* (no room for doubt) the profession of our faith *without wavering*; for He is *faithful* that promised".

—Heb 10:22

He is faithful that promised! Amen!

The Bible is the Source of the "Good News" of the Gospel
— part one —

The Bible is the only true source and explanation of God's plans and desires for mankind. The gospel of God is only found in the Bible. The word "gospel" means "good news" because our creator has good news to give us after He explains the bad news of our sinful condition. There are other so-called "gospels" among the religions and philosophies of men, but they are false gospels and not really good news at all because they cannot save anyone. What they all have in common is that they require man to contribute to his being made righteous. Being righteous is the state of being considered sinless in God's sight; and not only sinless but having done *everything correctly* as God demands through His law.

Some false gospels have no connection with Christianity and do not pretend to, like Islamism, Buddhism, and other world religions other than Christianity; but in the broad scope of what passes for Christianity are other false gospels like Mormonism, Seventh-Day Adventism, the Jehovah Witnesses, among many. Some are immediately evident as being false to those with even a cursory acquaintance with the Bible like Mormonism and Seventh-Day Adventism while others are more subtle and deceptive.

My point is not to name and explain every false gospel but only to mention major examples that claim to offer a path to God but in fact *do not*. Again, they all have the same thing in common—they either deny the Bible was established by divine authority and is the only revelation of truth from a singular true God, or they misunderstand what the Bible teaches.

The better strategy is to explain the Gospel as the Bible truly teaches it and then you can readily identify those that are false. In the world of finance bank tellers used to (before scanning machines) be required to study real examples of U.S. paper money. Since counterfeits come and go and each one is different it is more effective to study the genuine article than the counterfeits themselves. By becoming expert in the nuances of real currency one can spot the fakes. So what does the Bible say and what is the true gospel? Only by becoming expert at what God says about salvation can we spot the fakes.

Let me preface by saying that the scope of God's revelation to man is actually defined by the Bible itself. These parameters are declared by God in Revelation 22:18,19 and they are the Bible alone, no additions nor subtractions. The Bible is our complete authority and the truth which we must declare. We cannot add anything from outside the Bible or subtract anything from within the Bible when considering the Gospel and the God that gave it:

> "For I testify unto every man that heareth the words of the prophecy of this book, If any man *shall add* unto these things, God shall add unto him the plagues that are written in this book: And if any man *shall take away* from the words of the book of this prophecy, God shall take away his part out of the book of life, and out of the holy city, and from the things which are written in this book." —Rev 22:18-19

So the Bible in its entirety should be our only source of God-given authority. The heavens truly do reflect the glory of God, but you need to understand specifically who that God is.

First, you need to know that He is your Creator, and as a creature of the great Creator you are accountable for the life you lead. God, in His mercy has given us all that is needed for an eternal union and happiness with Him in His Scriptures. Paul writing to Timothy explained it well:

> "From a child thou hast known the Holy Scriptures, which are able to make thee wise unto salvation through faith which is in Christ Jesus. *All scripture is given by inspiration of God*, and is profitable for doctrine, for reproof, for correction, for instruction in righteousness: that the man of God may be perfect, thoroughly furnished unto all good works". —2 Tm 3:15-17

Always let the Bible instruct you, for it alone holds the gospel, which is the wisdom of God unto salvation. It alone can instruct us in righteousness. The schemes and teachings of men, their traditions and religions always include a prideful work effort which are considered filthy rags to God.

> "But we are all as an unclean thing, and all our righteousnesses are as filthy rags;..." —Is 64:6a

The problem is one of righteousness. Without it we perish eternally. We must be seen as righteous in order to enter into God's presence in Heaven.

> "For the Lord knoweth the way of the righteous: but the way of the ungodly shall perish." Ps 1:6

As we have seen before— being righteous is the state of *being deemed sinless in God's sight*; and not only sinless but having done *everything correctly* as God demands through His law. All our attempts at righteousness are considered filthy rags by God. They are repulsive foul things. The words filthy rags in the Hebrew of the Old Testament is an expression likened to used menstrual cloths.

So why are we not righteous? Because Adam was created in the image of God, to reflect the righteousness of God but that image and ability was destroyed by Adam's sin of breaking God's law.

"And the LORD God commanded the man, saying, Of every tree of the garden thou mayest freely eat: But of the tree of the knowledge of good and evil, thou shalt not eat of it: for in the day that thou eatest thereof thou shalt surely die." —Gn 2:16-17

"And when the woman saw that the tree was good for food, and that it was pleasant to the eyes, and a tree to be desired to make one wise, she took of the fruit thereof, and did eat, and gave also unto her husband with her; *and he did eat.*" —Gn 3:6

The nature of mankind was corrupted in Adam by his fall into sin and this corruption is transmitted to us because we are all descendants of Adam. As such we are sinners at birth, born into this world with hearts bent on disobeying the laws of God and then we go on to do just that— break His laws, all day long, every day. God says it concisely here:

"There is none righteous, no, not one. There is none that understandeth, there is none that seeketh after God. They are all gone out of the way, they are together become unprofitable; there is none that doeth good, no, not one." —Rom 3:10-12

So now we understand the bad news. We're unrighteous, and we have no power to change that.

The good news is that God foresaw our predicament and made a way to remedy it for all that would trust not in themselves but in Him only. The good news is of the person and work of Jesus Christ in saving men. It is the message of the incarnation of God the Messiah that came to mediate a way to peace with God. The good news of the gospel encompasses His resurrection and glorification which assures us of ours. The content of the gospel is entirely that of Christ; it includes none of us.

We must know: Who Christ is, what Christ has done, who He did it for, where He is now, and what He will do when He returns. The gospel announces that the kingdom you need to enter into is here. The gospel is the Word of God *properly* understood.

"When they were alone, He explained all things to His disciples". —Mk 4:34

The disciples had the kind of relationship with Jesus wherein He explained all that He was doing to them. They could not always receive it, but He did so nonetheless and often reminded them of things He had previously explained to them when they finally came to pass. You need to have this kind of relationship with Jesus. You must seek time alone to truly search the scriptures and find Jesus and His salvation message. The Holy Spirit will explain it to the humble heart. Anywhere you cut the Bible it will bleed Jesus, and as a preacher friend of mine explains: "the wind don't blow where the blood don't flow." Pray that the Holy Spirit's wind blows your way.

The gospel is only effectual in a person who is humble and understands the end of his own strength, and his inability to please God. The apostle Paul's name was changed from Saul to Paul by God. It means "small." God makes sure we understand that the gospel comes to the humble and only works in a man that understands how small he really is.

God has promised: "If you seek Him with all your heart, you will surely find Him."

The Bible is the Source of the "Good News" of the Gospel

— part two —

Previously, we saw that the Bible properly understood, teaches that salvation is entirely a work of God. It does not involve our will.

"He came unto his own, and his own received him not. But as many as received him, to them gave he power to become the sons of God, even to them that believe on his name. Which were born, not of blood, *nor of the will of the flesh, nor of the will of man,* but of God." —Jn 1:11-13

John makes it abundantly clear that the will of man is not involved in the power given by God by which men become sons of God. "Which were born...not...of the will of man, but of God." But if our salvation is not dependent upon anything we can do to make it happen how is anyone saved? The answer is that God is the initiator of salvation in every case. When a man shows the humility of heart to believe the things God has declared in the gospel, it is because God has initiated the work of salvation in that man's heart.

"And a certain woman named Lydia, a seller of purple, of the city of Thyatira, which worshipped God, heard us: *whose heart the Lord opened*, that she attended unto the things which were spoken of Paul." —Acts 16:14

So you see that it is the Lord that opens the heart of those who hear and attend to the words of the Gospel. Why then are some men saved and others are not? If it is not because some men freely chose to follow Christ by willing to do so while others do not, then how can we explain this? This question is at the heart of the issue, but the answer is clearly disclosed in God's Word. It was God's plan in eternity past, before the earth was even formed, to make a covenant promise between the Father and the Son in which the Father gave to the Son a group of people that would forever be His. These people were given to Christ as his inheritance. They were a gift from God the Father to Christ His Son, but because of the sin which condemned them, Christ had to redeem them by volunteering to die to pay for their sins because they could not do so for themselves.

"Everyone *the Father gives Me* will come to Me, and the one who comes to Me I will never cast out. For I have come down from heaven, not to do My will, but the will of Him who sent Me. This is the will of Him who sent Me: that I should lose none *of those He has given Me* but should raise them up on the last day. For this is the will of My Father that everyone who sees the Son and believes in Him may have eternal life, and I will raise him up on the last day." —John 6:37-40

The term that Scripture uses for these people that the Father gives to the Son are called the *elect* or those that have been *chosen* by God to be saved. This act of choosing some to be saved is called *election*; it is also variously called *predestination* in the Word.

"According as *He hath chosen us* in Him before the foundation of the world, that we should be holy and without blame before Him in love: *Having predestinated us* unto the adoption of children by Jesus Christ to Himself, according to the good pleasure *of His will,* to the praise of the glory of His grace, *wherein He hath made us accepted* in the beloved." —Eph 1:4-6

Does that not say it all! He did the choosing before the foundation of the world was made. He predestined us to adoption into Christ. He did it by virtue of the good pleasure of His will not ours; and it is He that has made us accepted (our being made righteous).

Our having been accepted is because we have been deemed righteous. It is His work not ours. The act of being made righteous is also called *justification* or the action of *being justified.*

While we are still dead and separated from God by our sins God initiates His saving work:

> "For when we were yet without strength, in due time Christ died for the ungodly....God commendeth his love toward us, in that, while we were yet sinners, Christ died for us. Much more then, being *now justified* by his blood, we shall be saved from wrath through him. For if, when we were enemies, we were reconciled to God by the death of his Son, much more, being reconciled, we shall be saved by his life." —Rom 5:6-10

This wonderful election and justification of God is totally unconditional, which means it is not based on anything that God saw in us that made us worthy of His choice. It is a choice made entirely by His good pleasure and not because there was anything good about us. As a result of His sovereign choice and work of regenerating us (giving us a new heart that yearns for Him) we surrender to His will unconditionally. There are no "ifs", "ands" or "buts",— his calling is irresistible.

> Calvin explains: "The grace of God does not find men fit to be chosen, but makes them fit".

> Augustine adds: "Man is converted not because he wills to be, but he wills to be because he is ordained to election".

A knowledge of these gospel truths creates humility within us. To know that there was nothing in us that warranted God's chosing us is humbling. Praise God that He has chosen to elect some.

It also gives us great insight into how we are to evangelize properly. We are freed from the temptation to use techniques of persuasion. The gospel is not something we must convince people of. It is not by clever argumentation that men receive the truth, but by the faithful working of the Spirit in those hearts that have been chosen to accept and respond to the truth of it. Knowing this allows us to rely on the assurance of God's Word to bear its fruit as He wills. This is liberating to us as we obey God in preaching the gospel faithfully to others. We can rest in His sovereignty. We are powerless, outside of the declaration of His Word, to bring anyone to faith. We need not sugarcoat the Word to make it more acceptable.

The great Protestant Reformation produced many notable mottos in Latin that express the truths about the gospel that the Reformers fought for. They are:

Sola Scriptura— The Bible Alone
Tota Scriptura— All of The Bible
Sola Gracia— By Grace Alone
Sola Fide— Through Faith Alone
Solus Christus— Through Christ Alone
Soli Deo Gloria— For God's Glory Alone

These truths sum up the highlights of the gospel and raise up our Savior to the highest throne, and keep Him there.

As Augustine wrote:

"Christ is not valued at all unless He is valued above all".

Have you valued Christ above all? Surely this is a time to have dealings with Jesus. Pray that God will make you as Christ in His eyes. Pray that His example of love, meekness and long suffering be reflected by your new walk. You can't learn this much of Jesus without knowing He must increase and you and your way must decrease. What does our world need right now? Does this world need more of you? No, it needs men and woman being conformed to the image of Christ:

"For whom He did foreknow, He also *predestined to be conformed to the image of His Son...*" —Rm 8:29

The Gospel is the light that reveals we are guilty sinners. The Gospel tells us that we are lost and that we are totally unable to save ourselves. The Gospel tells us that we have defaced the image of God. We hide from God and are under the dominion of sin and death, and in the grip of Satan. We must be recreated and come out from the dominion of sin. We must be rescued from the power of Satan and saved from the wrath of God. The true Gospel of Jesus Christ is the answer to mankind's problem of sin and separation from God. The Gospel meets man's most basic need, as it proclaims Christ as our solution. You know the bad news and you now know the good news. Do not believe those who will tell you that you can be saved by any work that you could do. You cannot will your salvation but the Gospel says:

"*Believe* on the Lord Jesus Christ, and thou shalt be saved..."
—Acts 16:31

And again it says:

"And this is His command: to *believe* in the name of his Son, Jesus Christ, and to love one another as he commanded us." —1 Jn 3:23 (NIV)

So— *believe* the good news of Jesus Christ!

Embrace the *"it's-already-done"* aspect of the true gospel, rather than the *"do-this-do-that"* requirements of religion; such works and doing have never saved anyone.

Christ said of His atoning work: "It is finished!" —Jn 19:30

It has been done completely, so—Rest in Him!

Let our Leaders and Saints Humbly Serve

In the book of Luke our Lord illustrates what's wrong with most of us today. In the midst of wondering who will betray Jesus there arises a dispute among the disciples as to which of them should be considered the greatest (Lk 22:24). Jesus explains that it's the world that behaves that way because it insists on Lordship. The source of such desires is revealed in verse 31— "Simon. Simon, behold, Satan hath desired to have you, that he may sift you as wheat."

Jesus tries to show that a true leader should serve while still esteeming the younger as the greatest. What does Jesus do next? He prays for Simon to strengthen his brothers, and that in the end his faith will prevail. And still, Peter denied Him before the rooster crowed the third time.

The disciples ask: Who is the greatest in the kingdom? (Mt 18:1) Jesus answers: "Whoever humbles himself as a little child."

The disciples disputed over who should be the greatest. (Mk 9:34) Jesus tells them: "If any man desire to be first, the same shall be last of all, and servant of all, and he took a child."

Then there arose a reasoning among them, which of them should be greatest. Again Jesus takes a child. (Lk 9:46)

In the washing of feet, Jesus gives us the pattern— Do as He has done!

Pride, willfulness, ambition, and even Satan constantly warring against humble service for our Lord. It's *mine* as opposed to it's *ours*.

> "He that is greatest among you shall be your servant, and whosoever shall exalt himself shall be abased; and he that shall humble himself shall be exalted." —Mt 23:11

James says;

> "God resisteth the proud, but gives grace unto the humble."
> —Jas 4:6

Take a moment and think back. Try to pinpoint some recent circumstance in which you insisted obstinately in doing the opposite of Jesus' example and commands. How has that worked out for you? As for me, it scares me. I can only be exalted according to my Savior's wisdom, and in His estimation. Less of me and more of Him, means just that.

The attack is on our church, and our ministries, and is old as Satan himself. He is going to and fro seeking those he can devour. The more you esteem your own worth, the broader he smiles. The more you put down a fellow saint the higher he is raised. The attack is not on the world, as Satan already enslaves it. The attack is on you and your church. A true church exhibits love for the brethren.

> "Finally, be ye all of one mind, having compassion one of another, love as brethren, be pitiful, be courteous." —1 Pt 3:8

The way up is always down.

Mercy and Grace

Mercy and Grace! Praise God for both. These are two of the most important concepts in all of Scripture and we must acknowledge that we owe our eternal life to them both. I'm curious though— Can you give a concise definition of each? Admittedly, they are similar and easily confused by many. They have been described as two sides of the same coin, and both are equally vital acts of God in salvation. So, if I may, I'd like to share with you the definitions I was taught early on in my Christian walk that gave me complete clarity to distinguish between them.

First, Mercy. Mercy is— *When we do not get what we do deserve.* So, what do we deserve? Well for one thing, we all deserve to receive the penalties for our sins. So when our righteous God makes a way to forgive us of our sins and withhold from us the penalties those sins deserve then that is what God calls mercy.

Grace on the other hand is— *When we do get what we do not deserve.* Now think about that. Think of all the things that a Christian has received that were completely undeserved. To begin, we did not deserve to have a relationship with God but He gave us one. We did not deserve to have a Savior but we were given Christ.

The word *grace*, comes from a root meaning "to bend or to stoop". A superior person condescends to an inferior when he displays an undeserved favor. He has stooped low to bestow such grace. In fact another common definition for grace is simply "unmerited favor".

The entire pre-flood world was found by God to be only committing that which was evil continuously in His eyes...

> "And God saw that the wickedness of man was great in the earth, and that every imagination of the thoughts of his heart was only evil continually". —Gn 6:5

God, with whom nothing is hidden from His knowledge, surveyed each and every living soul and concluded that man was *only evil continually.* In other words, nobody did anything good but rather *only* did that which was contrary to His will (law) *all the time*, and so He decided to destroy mankind...

> "But Noah found *grace* in the eyes of the Lord" —Gn 6:8

Thank God He had mercy on Noah and his clan (who deserved the same destruction as the rest of the world) and by grace (giving that which is undeserved) chose to bestow the free gift of salvation to those eight souls that entered the Ark by faith (a faith that was also a gift of grace).

God reiterates this dismal assessment of mankind elsewhere:

> "The Lord looked down from heaven upon the children of men, to see if there were any that did understand and seek God. They are all gone aside, they are all together become filthy: there is none that doeth good, no, not one". —Ps 14:2

The apostle Paul gives this indictment against the whole world again in the third chapter of Romans when he echoes Psalm 14:2 in his argument:

> "As it is written,— *There is none righteous, no, not one.* There is *none that understandeth, there is none that seeketh after God.* They are *all* gone out of the way, they are together become unprofitable; *there is none that doeth good, no not one."* —Rom 3:10

You see, we have a creator God who exists outside the boundaries of time. He is not subject to time as He is the very creator and Master of time itself. So God, who is cognizant of every deed of every man from the beginning of the creation of Adam and Eve until the moment He returns to judge the world, can and has already (in the Scriptures) declared that nobody is righteous! There never was nor will there ever be a single human being (except for Jesus Christ) that has done anything righteous. Every one of us is dead in our trespasses and sins and at enmity (in a state of hatred and animosity) unless and until God saves us by a work of grace.

When God saw me, He saw a dead man who hated him and by my choice, was his enemy; a slave of Satan. I had earned myself hell as the just punishment for my sins. But— Praise God! I found grace in the eyes of the Lord. He has chosen me in Christ, even before He laid the foundation of the world, that I should be holy and without blame before Him in love.

> "According as *He hath chosen us in Him before the foundation of the world*, that we should be holy and without blame before Him in love: *Having predestinated us unto the adoption* of children by Jesus Christ to Himself, *according to the good pleasure of His will*, to the praise of the glory of His grace, wherein He hath made us accepted in the Beloved. In whom we have redemption through His blood, the forgiveness of sins, according to the riches of His grace." Eph 1:4-7

I have redemption because of His blood, according to the riches of His grace.

> "And you has *He made alive*, who were dead in trespasses and sins....But God, who is rich in *mercy* (He didn't give me what I deserved), for his great love with which he loved us. Even when we were dead in sins, has made us alive together with Christ, *by grace* (He gave us what we don't deserve) you are saved. —Eph 2:1-5 (KJV2000)

And one of my favorite verses in all of Scripture—

"For *by grace* are ye saved through faith; and that not of yourselves: it is *the gift of God*. Not of works, lest any man should boast." —Eph 2:8-9

Did God see the apostle Paul seeking Him? Did Paul's seeking God have anything to do with God choosing him? No, Paul held the apostle Stephen's coat while they stoned him to death. In fact, Paul *never sought after God* (as God prescribes that we seek Him) Paul only sought after righteousness according to the law trusting in his own zeal for the "God" he thought he knew. Paul was actually on his way to kill more Christians,...but God who is rich in *mercy*, knocked him off his high horse and revealed Himself to Paul, saying— "Saul, Saul, why are you persecuting me?" —Acts 9:4

Jesus said it best in Jn 6:44:

"*No man can come* to me, **except** the Father which hath sent me *draw him*: and I will raise him up at the last day."

and,

"...this is the Father's will which hath sent me, that of all which He hath *given* me I should lose nothing, but should raise it up at the last day". —Jn 6:39

and,

"Ye have not chosen me, but *I have chosen you*." —Jn 15:16

and,... "for without me *you can do nothing*." —Jn 15:5b

You see, salvation is totally a gift of God's grace and a product of His mercy. He must do it *all!*

He must do the seeking. He must do the choosing. He must do the revealing of Himself. He must do the drawing. He must make the payment for sin! He must have mercy! As the hymn declares— "Jesus paid it all, all to Him I owe."

None of us were good, and none of us sought Him, until God, who is *rich in mercy*, showed us the same light He showed Paul.

We were created to give Him glory, not ourselves. He did it all, we didn't. He circumcised the foreskin of our heart by His grace. We couldn't. He sprinkled us with clean water. We couldn't. He took away our heart of stone. We couldn't. He loved us and made us to love Him! And isn't it easy, to love the only one who—

"...is able to keep you from falling, and to present you faultless before the presence of his glory with exceeding joy. To the only wise God our Savior, be glory and majesty, dominion and power, both now and ever. Amen. —Jude 1:24-25

Tough Words from Tough Saints

In 1 Peter, when the apostle speaks of suffering, he is not speaking of suffering due to our sicknesses or infirmities, but rather of sufferings that comes as a consequence of the opposition we receive from the world simply because we are Christians. In America, there is little real persecution of Christians (at this time at least). Sure, we've got the lefties and atheists that hate God and Christians and seek to have the Ten Commandments removed from courthouses and Christmas Trees from public places, but that is hardly the persecution the Scriptures have in mind.

All around the world, people are converting to Christianity, especially in Muslim countries and they are being arrested, tormented, beaten and killed because of Christ. Here in the U.S. many professing Christians barely speak up for what is true and righteous and rarely if ever take a stand that might jeopardize their friendships, family relationships, or employment.

Have you seen the bumper sticker that asks: "If someone accused you of being a Christian, would there be enough evidence?" Well, what do you think? Would there be enough evidence to convict you of being a Christian if Christianity were made a crime? How many hours of testimony could be brought against you? Or, would they throw the case out of court?

In the paraphrased words of Dr. Lloyd-Jones:

"The main trouble with the Christian church today is that she is too much like a clinic, too much like a hospital; while the world is going to hell outside! 'We are all suffering with the mumps and measles of the soul' (Charles Lamb) while feeling our own pulses. We have lost the concept of the army of God and the King of Righteousness in this fight against the kingdom of evil. Holiness is a matter of service, not of feelings and subjective moods. We are meant to be serving the living God with our whole being, not serving sin. We must not fraternize with the enemy. That is the New Testament's way of teaching holiness....Listen to the sergeant-major drilling and commanding his troops, warning, threatening, commanding, while showing what to do. The New Testament's teaching is altogether different from the sentimentality and subjectivity that have controlled holiness and sanctification teaching too long. It rather gives military commands: "Fight the good fight of faith," "Quit yourselves as men," "Put on the whole armor of God," "Stand in the evil day," No notion of clinic or hospital, but rather looking at things in terms of God and His Glory, and the great campaign, which He inaugurated through the Son of His love and which He is going to bring to a triumphant conclusion." —Martyn Lloyd-Jones, *Romans 6: The New Man*, pp. 173-175 (on Romans 6:13)

I believe these words are sobering, but not necessarily tough enough. Consider:

"Let us put away our own ideas and plans, and let the Lord work when and how he will. Let us look away from difficulties, unlikelihoods, impossibilities, and rest simply on the Lord. This honors him; and he will honor us. How much has faith done! How much it still will do!" —John Milne

"In an age of false ideals and hero-worship, it will be found good to make one who took, as his great model, both in service and suffering, the Son of God; who knew, above most, what intimacy with Him could do, in molding character, and in producing a true and telling life." —Horatius Bonar speaking of John Milne

Do you finally want to be effective for Christ? Do you want to leave behind enough evidence to convict you of being a Christian? Jesus gave the instructions and may have said it best in Matthew when He spoke:

> "For this reason I say to you, do not be worried about your life, as to what you will eat or what you will drink; nor for your body, as to what you will put on. Is not life more than food, and the body more than clothing? "Look at the birds of the air, that they do not sow, nor reap nor gather into barns, and yet your heavenly Father feeds them. Are you not worth much more than they? "And who of you by being worried can add a single hour to his life?" —Mt 6:25-27 (NASB)

You see, we are rendered ineffective for Christ because of our fears. We fear men's opinions of us, we fear rejection, we fear that doing the right thing will cost us. We worry about our life, and we make compromises accordingly. We worry that standing for Christ could cost us our job, and then how can we pay for everything we need to survive? But Jesus says that *He* is our provision, that He provides for the lowliest of creatures. They need not worry about their next meal because God provides for even the tiniest little birds we see eating our grass seed! The answer is to obey God and seek His glory. Seek His kingdom, trust His promises—

> "But seek first His kingdom and His righteousness, and all these things will be added to you. —Mt 6:33

Lord, Could it Be?

Gracious Heavenly Father,

We bow before you this morning, recognizing that the work you began in us, is still not complete. We need your continuing grace that we might do those excellent things you desire from us. We must make our calling and election clear, proving the fruits of our righteousness as we learn more and more about you from your holy Word. We are bowing to your perfect law of liberty, knowing that it matters to you that we grow in grace; no longer arguing with the truth, but declaring it.

We trust the means you have appointed— that being families united around your Word and taught by the examples of godly men and women demonstrating your truth in the Word, we may gain a heart of wisdom. We see the wisdom in your provision of the church and it's saints, and pledge to assist in it's purpose and unity. You are not distant, but you are here, with the church to whom you have entrusted the keys to your kingdom. We do not believe those who tell us— "Look! Here is wisdom", or "Here is Christ!" when they are not pointing us to your Word. We know as Paul did, that you are our protector, standing with us through the storm, and we must stay in the boat and trust you through our turmoil. Make our church an institution that loves your truth so people will become saved.

Our children must cling to the wisdom their parents hand down to them as we should cling to the wisdom you have given us from above. Help us to bear fruit in our evangelism, declaring your Word, having faith in it's power unto salvation. We have witnessed firsthand your faithful chastening for our sin and the forsaking of your prescribed methods. We know that such inventions of men are departures from wisdom and are always fruitless and self-serving.

Help our church understand that we *must* know our Lord and Master more intimately. The One who, in His great mercy, chose us before the foundation of the world. The One who paid the price that we could not. The One who loved an elect remnant and clothed her with His righteousness as He took upon Himself her sin. Let us give proper glory to God, never relying on our sin-stained works as worthy of anything but hell, as they are but filthy rags. Give us the grace to move our pride and ego to the side, making room for you to work in and through us; giving all the glory and honor to you who enables us to will and do that which is pleasing to you. We can do nothing apart from you, as we are only wise in You.

Help us to understand mercy and grace, and never minimize Christ's all-sufficient and complete work, on which we can never improve. Instead, may we be faithful to march to the orders of our King as we go into all the world making disciples and loving as He loved us. As children of God we are not our own— we have been bought with a great price. We must decrease—He must increase! May we be filled with the living waters that must flow into the parched dry ground of men's hearts. We remember that Christ humiliated Himself to become sin for us, so that we may live in righteousness to Him. As Paul tells us:

> "For if by one man's offense death reigned by one; much more *they* which *receive* abundance of grace and of *the gift of righteousness* shall *reign in life* by one, Jesus Christ. —Rm 5:17

We know that we can only effectively reign as co-heirs with You, our King, if we do what is required of such unworthy servants. We have been made stewards of your truth and wisdom; we know that you require us to be faithful!

"Moreover it is required in stewards, that a man be found faithful." —1 Cor 4:2

Father, please grant us an ever-growing love and dependence upon your truth. Grant us an ever-growing desire to know your wisdom—

"...you are pleased with truth in the inner person, and you will teach me wisdom in my innermost parts." —Ps 51:6 (ISV)

Lord, help us to see that your Gospel is your appointed means by which men will be saved. Help us to lean solely on the Gospel truths and not our own. May we trust your wisdom in faithfully preaching the Gospel to those who are lost; not compromising any of your truth. May we not soften it by removing its dire warnings or harden it by diminishing your willingness and ability to save those who embrace it in faith. It is the work of the Gospel we must do as we pray, preach and evangelize. Give us the strength to work hard today for we know that: "Night cometh when no man can work". (Jn 9:4) May we not be ashamed—

"For I am not ashamed of the gospel of Christ: for it is the power of God unto salvation to every one that believeth,..."
—Rm 1:16a

Amen.

We Must Shine
— part one —

"*Ye are the light of the world.* A city that is set on an hill cannot be hid. Neither do men light a candle, and put it under a bushel, but on a candlestick; and it giveth light unto all that are in the house. *Let your light so shine before men*, that they may *see your good works, and glorify your Father* which is in heaven." —Mt 5:14-16

Brothers and sisters— we can only shine forth the light of God to the degree that we model His holiness and righteousness. As we imitate Christ and obey Him we are like little lights that shine forth into this dark world. We are the candle but the flame and light is God's work in us. Apart from His holy fire being touched to our wick we have no light of our own. This light is entrusted to us.

I often wonder why must it be that we shine so little light? Sometimes I look at my own light and fear it's going to blow out altogether. Thank God that He keeps our feeble flames aglow. It is His work in us. There is no doubt though that some people consistently shine brighter than others and that even I shine brighter at certain times than at others. I see this as a function of faith. The Bible declares that—

"The just shall live by faith." —Rm 1:17b

This faith is our trust in the unseen.

> Now faith is assurance of things hoped for, *a conviction of things not seen.* —Heb 11:1 (ASV)

By faith we trust in unseen things but not in unknown things. Christians know their Father in heaven, but He is unseen. We believe in Jesus who reigns from heaven and yet He has been unseen by us. The tree of life is removed, and the temple torn down. All of these are out of our reach, and yet we have no doubt they existed.

The King James Bible renders this verse this way:

> "Now faith is *the substance of* things hoped for, *the evidence* of things not seen." —Heb 11:1

I love that. Faith is the very *substance* of things hoped for, and *the evidence* of things not seen. True faith is weighty, it has substance. It is the "stuff" of believing in unseen things. It is the evidence that these things really do exist beyond our physical realm. This faith is given to us as a gift from God. Without it we have no connection to the unseen things of God and His kingdom. We need to understand that this faith is not the kind of so-called "faith" that non-Christians have in their philosophies. Their faith, no matter how firmly or sincerely they hold it, can never be anything more than a mere wishing that what they are trusting in will turn out to be true.

They may be so convinced and confident in what they are hoping for that they may even be willing to die for their conviction, but that doesn't make what they are trusting in true or give their faith any real substance. They can have no genuine assurance. First, because they have a "faith", which by definition, is a trust in that which *will* fail them because it is false. Something false cannot be the source of real assurance.

But the eyes of the wicked shall fail, and they shall not escape, and *their hope shall be as the giving up of the ghost.*
—Job 11:20

The false hope of the unsaved will die with them. Their hopes of immortality by any means other than faith in Christ alone will perish with them.

Second, because the only true faith is given by God and has as its object a trust in the true things pertaining to the one true God. Our faith is not a mere "wishing" that what we are believing in will turn out to be true but our faith is a "knowing" that these things *are* true and trustworthy. Our faith is an *informed* hope because the certainty of these things we trust in is established by God. They will not fail and we will never feel the anguish and dismay someday (namely when we die) to find that our hope and affections were misplaced as the wicked will.

Through the wonderful gospel, the very power of God unto salvation, do we live and shine through faith—

"I have heard of thee by *the hearing of the ear* (the Gospel preached): but now mine eye seeth (faith) thee." —Job 42:3

"So then faith cometh by hearing, and hearing by the word of God." —Rm 10:17

The just shall live and shine by faith. Faith originates from God and is given to the believer who then manifests it by the new nature given to him by regeneration. Regeneration is the act whereby God changes our unsaved heart from what He calls a heart of "stone", which is hard and in rebellion to Him, and replaces it with a heart of "flesh", which is a softened heart that wants to love and believe God. With a new heart of flesh comes a new nature that is no longer at enmity (warring against) God but desires to do what God calls "good" and "righteous". The act of regeneration is entirely an act of God. He initiates it when He wills and to whom He wills.

He has not chosen to regenerate everyone and that is why most people will never come to faith in Christ and be saved. Only the just (those made righteous by justification—another act of God which accompanies the gift of faith), will live by faith. We shine brighter and brighter as we exercise our trust and obedience in Christ through faith.

"When the candle shined upon my head, and when *by His light I walked through darkness.*" —Job 29:3

We Must Shine

— part two —

What a wonderful thing saving faith is. It is a gift of God:

> "For by grace are you saved through faith; and that not of yourselves: it is the gift of God. Not of works, lest any man should boast." —Eph 2:8-9

Christ, the Faithful One, accomplished redemption for us. We understand our salvation came from His faithful obedience to the Father's will and plan. By this do we receive this faith given to us. No one can be justified by any work of their own. A god-given faith is the vehicle by which we are saved. God uses it so we may put our trust for salvation entirely in Christ. We must never forget that He that began this good work in us will be faithful to complete it. All credit goes to God for our perseverance in faith towards God. To the degree that we abandon thinking we can live for His glory through some inherent strength and ability of our own are we exercising real faith. For us to truly shine we need to daily abandon our own way of thinking and doing and be the slave/servant we were called to be.

Folks, it's time, this is the year, this is our calling. We must faithfully obey God and so shine forth His glory to a lost and darkened world. Someday we will see how often we failed. God forbid that we fail in grace, but we will see many missed blessings, and we may feel severe regrets. Will you look around to see who you could have warned, or what you could have done to God's glory. Will you be angry with yourself? I'm asking you now, as I also ask myself: "What are you doing of eternal worth?" Wake up and serve the God who died for you. You have a salvation to work out with fear and trembling. There are treasures to be stored in heaven. Don't say "Lord, Lord..." but not follow His commands. God warns us that trusting means we are to be doers of the Word and not just hearers only!

> "But be you doers of the word, and not hearers only, deceiving your own selves." —Jas 1:22

The book of Joshua tells us that those who rebel and harken not unto the word, shall be put to death.

> "Whosoever he be that does rebel against your commandment, and *will not hearken unto your words* in all that you command him, he *shall be put to death*." —Jos 1:18

King Josiah tore his clothes and feared the great wrath of God kindled against him and the people for not harkening to the word,

> "And it came to pass, when the king had heard the words of the book of the law, that he tore his clothes." —2 Kgs 22:11

The unsaved world will have their own excuses to make. These vain men disobey God because they are dead in their sins, and deaf to God's Words. We who are alive have no such excuses. Why should we who have been quickened to life by His Spirit appear just as these dead men? If you *can* see, but *don't*, and *can* walk, but *won't*— what excuse can you make? We who have inherited every good thing in Christ, must consider— how are we using these gifts? Blessings become a curse when we covet them to ourselves. Talent foolishly buried and not used for the kingdom fails. A light given should not be hidden under a bushel. Remember all that you had faith in. Now is the time to shine forth.

"For he knoweth vain men, he seeth wickedness....for vain man would be wise, though man be born like a wild ass's colt. If thou prepare thine heart, and stretch out thine hands toward him; If iniquity be in thine hand, put it far away, and let not wickedness dwell in thy tabernacles. For then shalt thou lift up thy face without spot; yea, thou shalt be steadfast, and shalt not fear: because thou shalt forget thy misery, and remember it as waters that pass away: and thine age shall be clearer than the noonday;

thou shalt shine forth, thou shalt be as the morning.

And thou shalt be secure, because there is hope; yea, thou shalt dig about thee, and thou shalt take thy rest in safety. Also thou shalt lie down, and none shall make thee afraid; yea, many shall make suit unto thee. But the eyes of the wicked shall fail, and they shall not escape, and their hope shall be as the giving up of the ghost." —Job 11:11-20

So to shine we must exercise faith, and to exercise faith we must remember the object of that faith is God. Since God is unseen our faith must be informed by that which can be seen and comes directly from God, namely His Word.

"Forever O Lord *thy word* is settled in heaven." —Ps 119:89

"Heaven and earth shall pass away, but *my word* shall not pass away." —Mt 24:35

The Word is eternal. It is the source of all truth and wisdom. The Word *is* the light and to the extent that we are "doers of the word and not merely hearers" then we shine forth that light to illuminate our path in this world—

"*Thy word* is a *lamp* unto my feet, and *a light* unto my path."
—Ps 119:105

Now John explains that this Word was God,

"In the beginning was the Word, and the Word was with God, *and the Word was God*." —Jn 1:1

and this light shined in the darkness, but the darkness could not overcome it—

"And the light shines in darkness; and the darkness overcame it not." —Jn 1:5 (KJV2000)

and the light was Christ, the light and life of men—

"In Him *was life*; and *the life* was *the light* of men." —Jn 1:4

The wisdom of Proverbs emphasizes that the Word of God is life:

"My son, *attend to my words*; incline thine ear *unto my sayings*. Let them not depart from thine eyes; keep them in the midst of thine heart. For *they are life unto those that find them*, and health to all their flesh." —Prv 4:20-22

"Keep the commandments *and live*." —Prv 7:2a

Read Ephesians regarding Christ in whom we trusted after hearing the word of truth (the Gospel)—

"In whom ye also *trusted, after* that ye heard *the word of truth, the gospel of your salvation*: in whom also after that ye believed, ye were sealed with that holy Spirit of promise."

So there we have it folks. Christ is the Word. The Word is Life. The Word is truth. Faith comes from hearing the Word and trusting the Word. This is the Gospel of our salvation. We are to exercise faith in our unseen God by obeying His revealed will in the Word which can be seen and to the extent that we do so we shine as lights in this dark world. This light is a lamp unto our feet and is the light that men are drawn to.

Will you be a light that will draw men unto Christ? Will you strengthen your faith by getting into His Word and living there; deriving life from it? Will you be imitators of the Word; of Christ?

Will you truly shine?

Tidbits To Ponder

These are a few of my favorite short but powerful thoughts. I've collected them through my reading over the years and want to share them with you. These are the kind of bumper stickers I'd like to see!

Hell is truth known too late.

For us to become like Him, He had to become like us.

Things that are holy are revealed only to men who are holy.
—Hippocrates

Pray as if works don't count. Work as if prayers don't count.

The poorer the church, the purer the church.
—W.C. Hazlitt

One can be coerced to church, but not to worship.
—George Harkness

The forces of good in the world are immobilized less by their adversaries than by their sleep. —EM Poteat

Whenever God erects a house of prayer, the devil always builds a chapel there, and twill be found, upon examination, The latter has the largest congregation. —Daniel Defoe

To the believer Jesus says— walk. To the unbeliever— come.
                              —Dr. Gabriel Otero

There is a difference in: believing in God, and believing God, trusting what He says.

The new is in the old concealed. The old is in the new revealed.
                              —Augustine

Religion has never bowed it's knee to Christ.

Ecumenical movement is designed to destroy Christ. They consult together and cast Him down.

Never argue the truth: declare it.

What is more important? Eternity or living 3 score plus 10 years?

The good news always begins with bad news.

Problem with evil is that it's real.

Family is a haven in a heartless world.

Fallacies do not cease from being fallacies because they become fashion.

Worship is giving God the glory for what He has done.

The earth has no sorrow that heaven cannot heal.

Christian life is preparing to die.

Born once, die twice. Born twice, die once.

Blessed is everyone who is not offended by Christ.

I am not what I want to be. I am not what I used to be.

The sting of any rebuke is the truth. —Benjamin Franklin

Truth matters! Ultimate truth matters ultimately.

Lord, if we don't know you, raise us from the dead.

Let not one go to hell without our arms wrapped around his legs.
                                              —Charles Spurgeon

One Last Thought...

Thank you dear friend for taking the time from your busy life to read my book. I hope that it has been a blessing to you. That's my prayer!

For my brothers and sisters in Christ, I trust that reading of our great God and Savior can only be an encouragement and a thrill. Even those portions that were challenging and required some self-examination will prove to have their perfect work in as much as you go back to God in prayer.

To my friends and relatives that do not know Jesus personally; who have not yet recognized your need for this perfect Savior who is able to do more than you could ever imagine to save you from your sins and bless you in this life— I am praying for you by name! I hope we will meet in Heaven someday if you trust Jesus Christ for the righteousness you'll need to enter in. Remember nothing in you can commend you to God. He requires perfect men and woman washed clean of their sins; and He will accept those who have abandoned all hope and effort at pleasing God through their own works.

Read your Bible. Seek God in prayer. Ask that He reveal Himself to you. Ask Him to save you! He is ready and able!

May God Bless you!

"For this cause I bow my knees unto the Father of our Lord Jesus Christ, Of whom the whole family in heaven and earth is named, That he would grant you, according to the riches of his glory, to be strengthened with might by his Spirit in the inner man; That Christ may dwell in your hearts by faith; that ye, being rooted and grounded in love, May be able to comprehend with all saints what is the breadth, and length, and depth, and height; And to know the love of Christ, which passeth knowledge, that ye might be filled with all the fulness of God. Now unto him that is able to do exceeding abundantly above all that we ask or think, according to the power that worketh in us, Unto Him be glory in the church by Christ Jesus throughout all ages, world without end. Amen!"

—Eph 3:14-21

Abbreviations for Bible Books

Old Testament

Am	Amos	Mi	Micah
1 Chr	1 Chronicles	Na	Nahum
2 Chr	2 Chronicles	Neh	Nehemiah
Dn	Daniel	Nm	Numbers
Dt	Deuteronomy	Ob	Obadiah
Eccl	Ecclesiastes	Prv	Proverbs
Est	Esther	Ps	Psalms
Ex	Exodus	Ru	Ruth
Ez	Ezekiel	1 Sm	1 Samuel
Ezr	Ezra	2 Sm	2 Samuel
Gn	Genesis	Sg	Song of Solomon
Hb	Habakkuk	Zec	Zechariah
Hg	Haggai	Zep	Zephaniah
Hos	Hosea		
Is	Isaiah		
Jer	Jeremiah		
Jb	Job		
Jl	Joel		
Jon	Jonah		
Jo	Joshua		
Jgs	Judges		
1 Kgs	1 Kings		
2 Kgs	2 Kings		
Lam	Lamentations		
Lv	Leviticus		
Mal	Malachi		

New Testament

Acts	Acts (of the Apostles)
Col	Colossians
1 Cor	1 Corinthians
2 Cor	2 Corinthians
Eph	Ephesians
Gal	Galatians
Heb	Hebrews
Jas	James
Jn	John
1 Jn	1 John
2 Jn	2 John
3 Jn	3 John
Jude	Jude
Lk	Luke
Mk	Mark
Mt	Matthew
1 Pt	1 Peter
2 Pt	2 Peter
Phlm	Philemon
Phil	Philippians
Rv	Revelation
Rom	Romans
1 Thes	1 Thessalonians
2 Thes	2 Thessalonians
1 Tm	1 Timothy
2 Tm	2 Timothy
Ti	Titus

THE MISSION OF GREAT CHRISTIAN BOOKS

The ministry of Great Christian Books was established to glorify The Lord Jesus Christ and to be used by Him to expand and edify the kingdom of God while we occupy and anticipate Christ's glorious return. Great Christian Books will seek to accomplish this mission by publishing Gospel literature which is biblically faithful, relevant, and practically applicable to many of the serious spiritual needs of mankind upon the beginning of this new millennium. To do so we will always seek to boldly incorporate the truths of Scripture, especially those which were largely articulated as a body of theology during the Protestant Reformation of the sixteenth century and ensuing years. We gladly join our voice in the proclamations of— Scripture Alone, Faith Alone, Grace Alone, Christ Alone, and God's Glory Alone! Our ministry seeks the blessing of our God as we seek His face to both confirm and support our labors for Him. Our prayers for this work can be summarized by two verses from the Book of Psalms:

"...let the beauty of the LORD our God be upon us, And establish the work of our hands for us; Yes, establish the work of our hands." —Psalm 90:17

"Not unto us, O LORD, not unto us, but to your name give glory." —Psalm 115:1

Great Christian Books appreciates the financial support of anyone who shares our burden and vision for publishing literature which combines sound Bible doctrine and practical exhortation in an age when too few so-called "Christian" publications do the same. We thank you in advance for any assistance you can give us in our labors to fulfill this important mission. May God bless you.

For a catalog of other great
Christian books including
additional titles of a
devotional nature
contact us in
any of the following ways:

write us at:
Great Christian Books
160 37th Street
Lindenhurst, NY 11757

call us at:
631. 956. 0998

find us online:
www.greatchristianbooks.com

email us at:
mail@greatchristianbooks.com

Made in the USA
Columbia, SC
11 February 2023

11719100R10109